What others are saying

"2012 marks 40 years in martial arts for me. After exposure to a number of high level teachers of various internal martial arts and Systema, I can say that Brad's presentations on tension and its manipulation and effect on balance and structure is, by a wide margin, the most direct useful and comprehensible explanation of the subject I've seen to date."

- **Al McLuckie,** Systema Instructor
    Fort Wayne, Indiana

"Brad's WarriorFit® is a brilliant workout system that anyone can follow, enjoy, and feel good doing. If you are a Martial Artist or into fitness and conditioning, you can benefit from WarriorFit."

- **Martin Wheeler,** Systema Instructor
    The Academy, Beverly Hills, CA

"Brad breaks things down without shattering the Systema wholeness of the art. He is an excellent teacher, a consummate professional. I look forward to training with him again."

- **Matt McCormick,** Systema Instructor
    Systema Dayton

"I don't think anyone who's met Brad needs to be convinced, but judging from the hour and a half I was there, I saw the Systema that I had hoped was out there. He is a real treasure for anyone in the area (I'm jealous) and I would go back in a heartbeat. My time was brief but these are guys I would choose to spend my time with and it was a gift to be welcomed there."

-James Underwood

"I came up to visit the Denver area for work and it was suggested that I needed to look up Brad Scornavacco and train with him while I was there. I have been training in Systema for a couple of years in Austin with Gene Smithson and Jonathan Hewitt. The partners at Brad's school were friendly and welcoming as was Brad. I'm already looking forward to my next visit to the area and another training session with Brad."

-Tom Gaussiran

"On the striking; you've just got to experience it to begin to understand it. I've never been hit as hard in an actual fight, not once. I've experienced hits as hard in my martial studies, but never with so little effort on the part of the hitter. I want to know how to strike that powerfully, that easily. "If you're really stoked about your ground game, you might wanna try it on him...make sure you take the opportunity to have Brad hit you."

-Jeffrey Keston, Indianapolis, IN

"I wanted to let you have much how impressed I am with the WarriorFit system you developed, and how much I've enjoyed using it! It's become a fixture in my gym bag and a regular part of my training. In particular I'm enjoying how comprehensive it is while allowing me to be as focused or as varied as I want to be in any given workout. If I want to focus on a type of workout or a particular section of my body I can put together a workout that suits me, and if I don't feel like doing anything particular at all I can just see what the system throws at me. Just as importantly, it's fun, and I have yet to find myself getting in a rut doing the same old routine like I used to when I was just lifting or running. This is definitely something I'll continue to use and explore as well as something I'll be adding to my regular Systema classes. Fabulous execution of an excellent idea - nicely done!

- **Lance Rewerts,** Systema Instructor
  Iowa Systema

Systema Revelations
Lessons of the Russian Martial Art

Brad Scornavacco

outskirtspress
DENVER, COLORADO

The opinions expressed in this manuscript are solely the opinions of the author and do not represent the opinions or thoughts of the publisher. The author has represented and warranted full ownership and/or legal right to publish all the materials in this book.

Systema Revelations
Lessons of the Russian Martial Art
All Rights Reserved.
Copyright © 2013 Brad Scornavacco
v2.0

Cover by Brad Scornavacco. All rights reserved - used with permission.

This book may not be reproduced, transmitted, or stored in whole or in part by any means, including graphic, electronic, or mechanical without the express written consent of the publisher except in the case of brief quotations embodied in critical articles and reviews.

Outskirts Press, Inc.
http://www.outskirtspress.com

ISBN: 978-1-4787-1780-5

Outskirts Press and the "OP" logo are trademarks belonging to Outskirts Press, Inc.

PRINTED IN THE UNITED STATES OF AMERICA

Table of Contents

Preface i
Foreword iii
Introduction... vii
My Systema Origin Story 1
We're Not Normal 4
Is It Work or Play? 7
I'm Gonna Fall... 10
The Willow Tree vs. the Ball 12
The Illusion of Balance 14
Memories Deceive 16
Is There a Plan? 18
The Instructor Trap 21
Move and Think.. 24
Yes You Can Watch, But Get on the Mat 27
Newbies 29
 Four Types of Systema Students... 31
Why People Quit... 35
The Kettlebell Controversy 38
The Kettlebell Controversy – Part 2 42
250 lb. Man Knocked Down with No Physical Contact 44
I Know Systema Works Because I'm Doing It Wrong 46

Ever Get That Funny Feeling?	48
Walking Through Fog	50
What about Resistance?	52
So Striking Is Love, Huh?	56
So Striking Is Love, Huh? Part 2	59
Striking Is Love, Part 3	63
Punch Like a Prius	65
The Reality of the Short Stick	67
Fighting...with Sticks	69
What, Just One Guy?	71
Bad Analogies	74
Bad Analogies, Part 2	78
Swim-stema	81
Swim-stema – Part 2: Six Lessons from the Pool	84
Swim-stema – Part 3	87
Explaining or Training	89
Explaining or Training – Part 2	91
What Are You Trying to Achieve?	93
Cirque du Systema	97
Improvised Knife Work	100
Don't Try To Escape What Grabs You	101
Everyday Gestures	104
For Black Belts Only?	106
Systema, Baby, Systema	109
The Most Dangerous Close-Range Weapon in the World	111
You Gotta Ask Yourself One Question	113
You Gotta Ask Yourself One Question – Part 2	115
Small People vs. Big People	118
Vanishing Martial Arts	121
Lessons from the Second City	123
Be Undisturbed	128
That Looks Fake!	130
Can You Be Too Soft?	134
Jack-of-all-Trades, Master-of-all-Trades	136

The Journeys of ~~Sergei~~ Socrates with Dan Millman 139
Martial Arts Myopia 142
iRenew? Really? Come on 146
Systema vs. (Insert Art) 148
The Systema Anti-Principles 151
Sweet Home Chicago 154
A Critique of Systema 156
What's Wrong with Systema? 162
Where Are All the Women? 166
Can Women Learn to Defend Themselves in Just One Day? 169
Women, Systema & Body Armor 172
Are You Ready for the Indy 500? 174
You Can Go Your Own Way 177
Systema Hubris 180
The Danger of Having a Martial Artist for a Father 182
How Can I Make Him See How Cool Systema Is? 185
Systema Magic 187
Martial Jazz 191
Wrestling Alone 196
The Future of Systema 198
Systema as Asymptote 201
I Can't Make This Stuff Up 204
Systema Everywhere 212
Quotes from Class 214
Acknowledgements 217
About the Author 221

"What thou seest, write in a book..."
Revelation, 1. 11

It was six men of Indostan
To learning much inclined,
Who went to see the Elephant
(Though all of them were blind),
That each by observation
Might satisfy his mind.
The First approached the Elephant,
And happening to fall
Against his broad and sturdy side,
At once began to bawl:
"God bless me! — but the Elephant
Is very like a wall!".
The Second, feeling of the tusk,
Cried: "Ho! — what have we here
So very round and smooth and sharp?
To me 't is mighty clear
This wonder of an Elephant
Is very like a spear!"
The Third approached the animal,
And happening to take
The squirming trunk within his hands,
Thus boldly up and spake:
"I see," quoth he, "the Elephant
Is very like a snake!"
The Fourth reached out his eager hand,
And felt about the knee.
"What most this wondrous beast is like
Is mighty plain," quoth he;

"'Tis clear enough the Elephant
Is very like a tree!"
The Fifth, who chanced to touch the ear,
Said: "E'en the blindest man
Can tell what this resembles most;
Deny the fact who can,
This marvel of an Elephant
Is very like a fan!"
The Sixth no sooner had begun
About the beast to grope,
Than, seizing on the swinging tail
That fell within his scope,
"I see," quoth he, "the Elephant
Is very like a rope!"
And so these men of Indostan
Disputed loud and long,
Each in his own opinion
Exceeding stiff and strong,
Though each was partly in the right,
And all were in the wrong!

MORAL.

So, oft in theologic wars
The disputants, I ween,
Rail on in utter ignorance
Of what each other mean,
And prate about an Elephant
Not one of them has seen!

- John Godfrey Saxe

Preface

"Unfortunately, no one can be told what the Matrix is. You have to see it for yourself."
-Morpheus, The Matrix

"I know it when I see it"
-Justice Potter Stewart

"Systema, Russian Martial Art? What is it?"

I've been trying to answer this question, asked by prospective Systema students, since the day I began teaching it.

Sometimes I resorted to simple analogies like, "it's Russian Karate."

Other times I took the "what it's not approach:" no belts, no techniques, no kata. That never worked because people asked again, *"so what is it then?"*

Or, I tried to explain how Systema is used, by the Russian Special Forces.

| i

Or, by Systema's main principles, what it's based on. I talked about the breathing, the relaxation, movement and body alignment and how these simple principles gave rise to effective self-defense without memorized techniques.

I even appealed to Systema history — being attacked from all sides and developing a free and adaptive fighting method.

No explanation ever helped.

Then came YouTube. I stopped trying to explain Systema, opting to show people instead. That turned out worse than trying to explain Systema. Comments ranged from, *"that looked fake,"* to *"why are they letting that guy hit them?"* to *"that wouldn't work,"* and *"that looked rehearsed,"* coupled with quizzical looks. People still didn't understand Systema after watching my teachers perform it at the highest level. Sigh.

More effective than hearing about Systema, more effective than watching it has been getting students on the training floor — experiencing Systema. Even then, it takes a few weeks for most people to begin to see the big picture of Systema.

This book chronicles my attempts to teach Systema to those who have decided to try to understand it. Ultimately though, *"Systema can't be explained; it can only be experienced."*

Foreword

On Tuesday, July 10, 2007, I met Brad Scornavacco. I *thought* I was going to *discuss* training in Systema, but when I walked into the school and introduced myself, he asked "are you ready for class?"[1]. I said sure, as long as street clothes are ok. Ten minutes later I was *training*. I learned I didn't know how to do push-ups (in spite of, ostensibly, having done them for years). Twenty minutes after that, I was lying on my back, watching Mike (the German) stab a metal training knife at me so I could move from the touch.

At the end of class, I signed up (there were two other first-timers there that night, I haven't seen them again), and over the next several weeks, I was introduced to, among other things, 20, 30, and 40 count push-ups, doing squats while standing on my partner, and being hit by these odd looking strikes that came out of nowhere, and rattled my very essence. I loved every minute of it[2].

As I continued to study Systema with Brad, I began to understand why he loves the art, and why he's so good at teaching it. Some of the highlights are:

- Bachelor of Arts in Philosophy and Economics from Northwestern University
- Advanced Black Belt in Ed Parker's American Kenpo Karate under Lee Wedlake
- Systema Instructor Certificate from Vladimir Vasiliev

I know he also has extensive experience in Brazilian Jiu-Jitsu, Tai Chi and Filipino Martial Arts (Escrima, Arnis, Kali). Since he's studied and practiced different martial arts from different countries and cultures and *from different instructors,* he's seen many different techniques and methodologies from both a student and an instructor's point of view. When you combine that experience with his rigorous academic training, and his innate curiosity, you get someone interested in finding underlying concepts, teaching that as a foundation, and layering skills on top. To paraphrase from "4 Types of Systema Students", combining techniques with Systema is a powerful combination. You also get a teacher who never stops refining his teaching techniques; constantly searching for or coming up with new drills, explanations, and exercises to make sure that he has a way to reach every student.

This book is pulled from that research. As such, it contains sections on teaching, learning, starting, feeling, and explaining Systema. Are you a new instructor, or running a training group, and need a good way to ramp up the speed in order validate your fellow student's skills? Check out "Are You Ready for the Indy 500". Have you been training in Systema for a few years and have good grasp of the basic concepts, but still have some issues around working full speed against a highly aggressive and tense attacker (this was a major sticking point for me, and I've discovered it seems to be a pretty common plateau)? Take a look at "What About Resistance" and "Small People vs. Big People" (read it even if you're a big person). Finally, if you've been training diligently, and you seem to have reached a plateau, read "The Systema Anti-Principles", "A Critique of Systema", and "What's wrong with Systema". I guarantee you will come away with a deeper understanding of the core principles, a new perspective on your current level and what you need to do to improve.

It's been slightly more than five years since I walked into Systema Colorado. In that time, I've worked to internalize, and make my own, Systema. I've been successful in some areas, and am still working in others. I don't think I'll be finished any time soon. One constant is I will be referring to the chapters in this book at least once a year, and probably more. I'm very happy that this information is now available to the entire Systema community.

- Paul Trout, Systema Assistant Instructor,
  Longmont, CO - 2012

Footnotes:
1. See "Yes, you can watch, but get on the mat!"
2. See "We're not normal"

Introduction

"Everything that needs to be said has already been said. But since no one was listening, everything must be said again."
— Andre Gide

Revelations and insights, such as the ones in this book, rarely occur in a neat, linear order. As such, you do not have to read this book from first page to last. You can pick it up anywhere, read a chapter and glean nuggets of knowledge as it suits you.

On a macro level, Systema is a mosaic. In each class, you work on one piece of the larger picture. You may not yet see the entire picture or see how the piece you have today fits into the whole. Yet, as you gain more and more pieces and more and more knowledge, the entire picture of Systema will become apparent.

At its core, Systema is a hologram; its totality is contained in each sliver of the art. If you tear a hologram in half, you don't lose half of the image. You can still see the whole image no matter how small you slice the hologram. Likewise, when you focus on learning and improving one piece of Systema, the entire art should still be expressed. All Systema principles apply to each topic. You should apply each lesson you learn to every aspect of Systema as you work.

Systema Revelations is a compilation of years of reflections and personal insights into this unique martial art as taught by Mikhail Ryabko and Vladimir Vasiliev. Many of the topics covered are the direct result of teaching Systema seminars and responding to my students' struggles to grasp the core principles of Systema. These revelations are part of my efforts to guide them along the path to proficiency. Along the way, there have been many opportunities to extend the lessons outside the training floor into the real world.

All of the opinions expressed in this book are my own; I make no claim to speak for my teachers or their views of Systema. I trust that you will take the ideas and lessons and form your own opinions as well based on your experiences. The individuality and personal expression of Systema is what attracted me to it, and helping you find, and cultivate, your Systema is a primary goal of this book.

My Systema Origin Story

Of the common human values, freedom is pretty high on my list. When I moved to Colorado in 1997, after training in Kenpo et al since 1984, and opened my own martial arts school, I felt free to explore any martial art I could get my hands on, and I did. Upon arriving in Colorado, I checked out the Kenpo scene, met and trained with some very high-level Silat teachers and continued to get into the MMA/ground-fighting craze. I was doing the standard JKD/cross-training thing and as part of that I wanted to continue my weapons training in the Filipino martial arts. I had a friend and teacher, Al McLuckie, who I met through my Kenpo teacher, and immediately invited him to come out and teach at my school. (Al has an excellent reputation in Filipino and Kenpo circles.)

I first met Al in Chicago when I was a kid training at Dragon Wind Kenpo Karate with Lee Wedlake. When I moved to Florida to train at Mr. Wedlake's new school in Fort Myers, Al frequently flew down to teach Filipino martial arts seminars and we re-connected. I thoroughly enjoyed learning and working with Al and looked forward to every training session. I knew that I wanted to train more with Al and put some intense effort to master his weapons work. In 1998, I brought Al to Longmont for a seminar on stick and knife work. I had been training in Filipino arts with Al, Huk Planas of Kenpo fame as well as seminars, including some taught by the late Edgar Sulite and martial arts legend Dan Inosanto. I knew Filipino arts and what Al showed that day was definitely something *strange* and *different*. I loved it!

After the seminar we were having dinner in Boulder and Al told me he had a confession to make. He was hesitant about what he was about to say because he was afraid I wouldn't have him come back to teach. He prefaced his confession with the fact that he lost students because of what he was about to tell me. Here I am waiting for the worst, but really intrigued. Al's big confession was that he wasn't teaching me Filipino martial arts, he was teaching Russian Martial Art!

I just about laughed in his face, because I couldn't really care less what he was teaching or where it came from — it was incredible! I had been on this mixed martial art path, the take-the-best-from-every-art kind of thing, but I knew that something didn't seem quite right about that idea. I was trying to go beyond techniques, not to just learn more of them and have my brain fight about which technique from which art I should use while under attack. I was at that *"there has to be something more than this, something that makes this all click"* point of my training. I also realized that my current training was yielding diminishing marginal returns, an economics term meaning that I was getting less and less skill out of more and more effort.

I knew Al was experiencing the same diminishing returns in his training too, so that when he came out of nowhere with a quantum leap in skill and martial arts ideas I knew something was up. I remember thinking to myself, *"where did all this come from"?* His revelation explained it.

An interesting aside to this tale is that a noted Indonesian martial artist attended a few of Al's seminars and loved everything Al taught, until Al said it wasn't Filipino, but Russian. He abruptly stopped training and went back to what he knew while, oddly, writing an article in Black Belt Magazine about the value of relaxation in training. After seeing his reactions to Systema, I understood Al's fears of losing students. Again, my view was *"who cares what you call it, it works."*

Al told me his Systema story and pointed me to Vladimir Vasiliev who I found out had a few Systema instructional VHS tapes available. I ordered everything he had that Monday morning. When the tapes came in the mail I literally watched each tape one right after the other. I couldn't get the next tape in the VCR fast enough. When I had watched every one, I started over. I did this at every opportunity for the next week.

After I had bombarded my brain with Systema, and started dreaming it, I started teaching Systema in all my classes. I stayed late and started scheduling extra classes and seminars just to have the chance to keep working it. I hadn't even met Vladimir at this point and already knew I would do whatever it took and pay whatever price to excel at Systema.

Then I met Vladimir, which is a story in itself!

We're Not Normal

I mean it, we're not normal. It took me awhile to realize it, but it's true. I used to think that *everyone* would love Systema when they saw it, and especially once they took a class. Who wouldn't? Well, my illusions have long since been shattered — for the better.

- If you're training Systema, you know what I mean.
- If you are even remotely interested in Systema, you kind of know what I mean.
- If you are a layperson, you probably don't get it.
- If you are a self-proclaimed "tough guy" from another martial art, you really don't get it.

Whatever the case, it's cool with me. I have moved on to acceptance of people's martial arts training choices.

I heard a friend talking about the founding of Starbucks Coffee recently. Don't worry, I'm going somewhere with this.

He said, *"Imagine being in this meeting. We're going to charge 5 bucks for a cup of coffee, open thousands of stores, give all the coffee exotic names so you need a dictionary to figure out what you are ordering, and make people wait for 10 minutes to get the darn thing.*

'Ok, I'm in. Who do I write the check to?'"

It's crazy to hear Starbucks' business plan explained because you can get a cup of coffee at Dunkin' Donuts for like a buck. Who in their right mind would pay five bucks for a cup of coffee? As it turns out, millions of us.

Now, imagine being in this martial arts instructor meeting:

"Ok, we're going to throw away all the belts and uniforms so no one can figure out just what they've learned or what they need to know.

Same with any testing — there are no belts and no testing.

Throw out any identifiable curriculum or teaching plans.

Ditch all the techniques and forms.

We're going to teach by — get this — hitting students with sticks, whips, chains and swing real knives and swords at them.

Oh, and we're going to have students stand there while we punch them until they puke, or want to.

But wait, we are going to practice slowly, without all the yelling and machismo so typical of martial arts. We're going to have everyone smile instead.

'Where do I sign up?'"

See the connection? We're not normal.

I find it humorous that the big, tough martial artists always reply to demonstrations of Systema striking with the, *"I'm not going to stand there and let someone punch me"* line. This is true even with punches from little old me.

They are normal. Afraid. Normal.

Of course, those of us who do stand there and let people punch us readily see and feel the value of it for training...a confidence and power that goes far beyond "normal."

Normal=Average=Mediocre="the herd." Blech! This is not us.

The challenge for us is to simultaneously walk away from the crowd and understand why they won't follow — and be content with this understanding. You can't walk away from the crowd and expect to be part of it at the same time.

Accept it. Be content with it. For Better or for Worse...We are not normal. We are *"Abby-Somebody." (To quote Igor in Young Frankenstein)*

Is It Work or Play?

"We don't stop playing because we grow old; we grow old because we stop playing."
- George Bernard Shaw

In Systema, we routinely refer to practice as "doing the work." But, we also instill a sense of "play" into practice.

So which should it be? Which is the right training mindset? Well, it's my favorite answer: both.

First, work. My teachers are/were military professionals who have to maintain a cool detachment while doing their job — the work. Once, in the forests of Russia a group of us were around a campfire late at night, Americans and Russians, when one of the Russians asked us this question,

"Now that you know us, what would you do if you were in battle and saw one of us coming at you, on the other side of the conflict? Would you shoot us or let us go?"

Obviously, emotions ran high that night. The answers ran the spectrum, but the questioner finally said, *"I would have to shoot you. It's my job."* (It is not personal.)

This is the element of work. If someone attacks you or your loved ones, it is your job to deal with the situation and resolve it. Vladimir uses the term "professionally," while I like to also say "clinically." You will see this sense of detachment among high-level Systema practitioners, in part, because it keeps emotions in check and allows us to act in ways that others can't even see.

On the other hand, you should enjoy your work. This is where play comes in training. Note I said, "in training." I wouldn't be playful with someone attacking my family, by any means. However, the best way to improve your skill is to explore and play with your partners in class.

Play is not self-conscious. Self-consciousness is something Vladimir speaks against when he says, *"don't care about what you look like."* If you want your body to react instantaneously and properly this attitude of play is crucial to training.

I had a woman come to class recently, expecting a typical martial art. After participating in a class she said, *"This is just like when I used to play around with my brothers as a kid."* One innate element of childhood play is to prepare kids for defending themselves as adults. If this drive, to practice defending ourselves playfully as children, works so well then why do we not continue to train the same way as adults?

The only answer I can think of is that adults think that having selfless fun is only for children. People think self-defense is serious business with no room for playing around. They are wrong. Stuart Brown, author of Play, says that play enables us to create, to solve problems, be happier, be smarter and more resilient. According to Brown, *"the opposite of play is not work, it is depression."*

I'm Gonna Fall

That was the cry that I heard from a diminutive young girl on my way back from vacation Monday. I told this story in class yesterday but it bears repeating.

Karla, Siena and I were in Dallas on the monorail going from one terminal to the next when these two girls hopped aboard. Apparently they'd never been to the "Big City" nor ridden a train before. So there they stood, in the middle of the train, holding on to nothing. The train jerked forward as we departed the terminal and they stood there like deer in the headlights, not knowing what was going on or that a monorail is unstable.

The larger of the two started repeating, like a mantra that would keep her upright, *"I'm gonna fall. I'm gonna fall."* I couldn't help but notice and laugh because her feet were *rooted* to the floor and she was swaying like a willow tree. In this comical instant I muttered under my breath, "Move your feet."

Maybe she heard me or maybe her body figured out what her brain could not, but she took a few steps and sat down.

Crisis averted. Whew! It saved me from having to catch her like I had to do once in Chicago many years ago. Back then, this other girl didn't move her feet and was in the process of falling on her head when I reached out, gently caught her and stood her back up before she even realized she was falling. The look of pleasant surprise on her face was priceless.

This little scenario reminded me of Systema class because so many problems can be overcome by taking a step or two. It's odd that so many martial arts go out of their way to teach people to "root" when everyone plants their feet instinctively once they've left childhood behind.

So, don't just stand there, take a step and adjust as you go, but get moving. Anywhere is better than where you are when you are in danger.

Well, most times.

The Willow Tree vs. the Ball

Mike Wurm asked me what country girls on a train have to do with Systema, so here's a further clarification.

A common martial arts analogy is to bend like the willow tree, and it's a good one — to a point.

I understand that it's better to bend like the willow tree than to break like the oak tree. But whenever I hear someone use this analogy, the first thing that comes to mind is to take an ax and strike at the trunk, where the tree is bending. That'd take it down.

Likewise, when you gyrate your upper body and don't move your feet when under attack, expect to be struck at this point of tension and either have your leg broken or be knocked down. I often see this when students do the basic Systema pushing/yielding drill. The aggressor pushes their chest and, in response, they move their shoulder and twist at the waist. This movement usually is not enough to dissipate the tension, which travels down their legs into their knees, the next vulnerable body part. I learned this lesson first-hand when Vladimir pushed my knee and easily knocked me down.

Now the willow does the best it can within its constraints as a tree, but there's a better way to look at your Systema training.

Vladimir proposes moving like a ball. The ball, unlike the willow, moves when force is applied to it. There is no fulcrum and no point of tension to take advantage of. I imagine those crazy, giant balls in the water from the old Prisoner TV show. The ball also maintains its form as it moves by rolling, as should you by moving your feet (I don't mean do cartwheels when moving like a ball). In the pushing/yielding drill, this means not letting the tension develop at your knee by simply picking up your foot or moving your leg in place.

So, root like a tree and get chopped down or move freely like a ball and defend yourself effortlessly. This "ain't" The Matrix.

Better yet, move like a person. Take a walk.

The Illusion of Balance

Balance is often seen as an ideal state to achieve, "you must have balance, balance is key," as Mr. Miyagi said. However, we spend most of our lives *out of balance*.

Imagine being on a boat. The "ground" under your feet is perpetually unstable, swaying with the ocean waves. You must shift your weight constantly to avoid falling overboard.

Now imagine being on land. The ground under your feet is moving because the earth is rotating. Of course, this movement is all but imperceptible, giving you the illusion of stability. Regardless, your body is still constantly shifting its weight and tension to prevent you from falling over.

Close your eyes and relax. You will feel your body rocking to adjust and re-align itself to the pull of gravity. If you can't feel it on two legs, stand on one leg and close your eyes.

Your eyes are one of the main ways that your body orients itself to your surroundings, which seem motionless. At sea, the surroundings are in obvious motion, making orientation a bit trickier and causing sea-sickness.

Even though you are on land, imagine that you are training

while at sea. You can't "root" or plant your feet. You must move your feet and shift your weight to stay standing. You must also be light on your feet and ready to shift in an instant.

Your body should feel like a buoy bobbing in the ocean waves. If you can elicit this feeling in your body, you'll move free and easy. And you won't be concerned about balancing on one spot.

Balance is really *dynamic imbalance,* or constantly transitioning your weight while maintaining control of your body.

Memories Deceive

Memories deceive. They outright lie to you and chain you to the past, rather than helping you to perform in the present. I "re-learned" this lesson on a few separate occasions over the past couple of weeks.

Let me explain.

Most New Systema students come to class stiff and rigid. I spend considerable effort to teach them how to relax and move. Once they're loose, I generally think they've got it. With an experienced student, my default mentality goes from "this guy is stiff" to "this guy will move." After all, I know he understands Systema and will react accordingly to force.

That assumption isn't true, and it shouldn't be.

The old Greek saying that *"you can never step in the same river twice"* rings true and applies to people. The person attacking you is not the person who attacked you yesterday, nor is he the person who has attacked you for years. The attacker in front of you today has been influenced by events and thoughts since the last time you met and is a different person, one who just looks like the person you knew.

This topic occurred to me because recently I've noticed that a couple of students who would usually be relaxed and mobile have become rigid and immobile.

Teaching a concept or move is different from just moving and reacting to threats. I find myself regularly having to show specific work to students to help them learn. I like to find an attacker who can assist who I don't have to loosen up or possibly hurt just to demonstrate a move.

The danger here — which I discovered — is that my memories of these students project into the present and to *expectations* of how they will act and move today. I noticed myself getting nonchalant with my moves and a bit lazy until the shock and surprise that the experienced students weren't moving like experienced students. I could feel my whole body and senses immediately wake up and change to the new information accordingly.

The immediate feedback of an experienced student now being more tense and rigid than usual instantly pulled me into the present moment, responding to "what is" versus "what was." I could now throw out whatever I was trying to teach and "Get to Work." Sure it made me feel better, but the new students missed the point.

What is the lesson?

Breathe, relax and stay open to the information an attacker is giving you right now. Throw expectation and anticipation out the window. People will always surprise you, so read their signals and be ready for anything. You can sort out why they went from loose and mobile to rigid and struggling later, after they are on the ground.

And, if you find yourself saying, *"Well, it worked last time,"* drop down and do 10 push-ups.

Is There a Plan?

"Engage the enemy and see what happens."
-Napoleon Bonaparte

I get this question all the time. Steve Burczyk always laughs, when during the end circle another student comments about how well organized the class was. So, how can class be so well-planned when I always ask students if there is anything in particular they would like to work on?

The answer is twofold:

First, yes I have a plan. I often choose topics and skills I would like to teach in class that day. What I bring to class as a teacher is the big picture. It is the over arching theme. I have several exercises and drills in mind to teach in that class.

Second, my plan is what I call rigidly flexible. After the warm-ups are finished and we move on to drills and exercises, I look around at all of the students to look for common mistakes or challenges.

At this point, I can change the course of the class, based on the student's needs that particular class. This works because I can draw on decades of teaching experience to structure a teaching curriculum at will. I don't recommend this for new instructors, who may just move on to teaching something different for variety's sake instead of for the student's sake. New instructors should have a solid lesson plan for class and refrain from winging it.

My ability to structure a class, based on this method, gives us an insight into learning Systema. Systema requires students to react spontaneously and instantaneously to various attacks. However, students must have background-knowledge of strategies and tactics to draw upon.

I see this every day teaching new students the martial arts. One of the easiest lessons to teach newbies is how to loosen up and move around. Evading and avoiding attacks is something people learn quickly, but it is not the ultimate sign of Systema skill.

The challenge comes when new students try to knock, or take down their attackers. This is when they hesitate. They move correctly initially but they have no experiences to draw upon to continue their counter attack. This is one advantage that students who have already studied martial arts have when learning Systema. These students have background knowledge and martial arts experience to draw upon. They just have to learn not to force it.

In the end, I teach very systematically:

- First, I begin.
- Second, I notice what is working and what is not working,
- Third, I change my approach to succeed.

This short lesson not only applies to Systema, it's a good rule of thumb to succeed at anything. The lesson is to adjust, reformulate, and respond instantly because, *"All plans change on contact."*

The Instructor Trap

Let me take you back several years to a head-scratching conversation I had with another Systema Instructor. At the time of this conversation, being a Systema Instructor meant that you were a rare breed, as the art hadn't exploded yet.

One way or another, talk turned to my school and how it was doing. I mentioned that things were hopping and that a fellow Instructor, and long-time friend, was coming to town to teach a seminar (then we were hitting the slopes).

Here's the head-scratching part...His reply? *"Why are you having him come teach? You're an instructor."*

I blew it off and moved the conversation to a different topic, but the implications of that comment have stayed with me until this very day (coming up on a decade later).

Here is the barrage of thoughts that ran through my head upon hearing this, in no particular order.

For one, it's my school and I'll have whomever I want come teach. If he didn't like this other instructor, he didn't have to come (he didn't).

I know this instructor I spoke to was trying to build a name for himself in the Systema community (which he has since done) and felt threatened, as if I should have him teach my students instead of someone else (I've never done this for various reasons).

Recent discussions with long-time instructors and students, led me to recall this head-scratching conversation and leads me to my final point:

Why would I have another Systema Instructor teach at my school if I were an instructor, and one of the first in America? My instructor certificate is so old it doesn't even have an expiration date on it.

Well, part of the answer lies in these recent discussions about what it means to be a Systema Instructor...just like all the debate about "what's really a Black Belt." As it turns out, I've had students and fellow long-time instructors have their own head-scratching encounters with some "certified instructors" and what they considered a lack of ability or knowledge of key principles on the part of these guys.

My point is not to debate who deserves what certification or designation. People can do whatever they want and they usually do, however mindlessly. **My point is this, I chose to, and still choose to, have another instructor come teach at my school because *they make me better.*** However, many Systema instructors unwittingly fall into "the instructor trap."

The first Instructor Trap springs when someone gets "the certification of instructor," and thinks he knows all there is about Systema and stops growing and challenging himself. We must continually challenge ourselves and go beyond our comfort zones to prevent stagnation and improve our skills, especially with the tag, Instructor, pinned on us.

The second Instructor Trap springs once someone becomes "an instructor" and stops being a student. He winds up surrounding himself with people of inferior skill (his students and other newbies) and stagnates. I choose to surround myself with people of near-equal or superior skill for the simple fact...*you become like the people you surround yourself with.* Being with Mikhail, Vladimir or other skilled instructors is like getting "a booster shot" of Systema skill and ideas for improvement.

The third Instructor Trap springs when an instructor insulates himself from new ideas. I've seen instructors build a myopic comfort zone of skill around themselves — whatever aspect of Systema they are good at — to the exclusion of learning anything else. Years ago, one instructor commented (after hearing about a Systema ground-fighting workshop) *"There's no ground-fighting in Systema"*?! What?! Pick almost any montage of Vladimir working and you will see tons of ground-fighting. Hello? One of his first videos was called Fighting from the Ground.

I'm always stretching my boundaries and, similarly, I know other instructors who are exceedingly creative with their Systema and training. They may show one idea that leads me to create six months worth of training ideas and classes. I welcome the input. On another note, it's exhausting being the guy at the head of the room all the time, teaching full-time as I do. It's refreshing to have someone else teach.

That's why I have other instructors teach at my school (even though I'm an instructor). My take-away training tip for you is, as I mentioned, surround yourself with the best people you can, and while they're around learn as much from them as you can.

If you find yourself being the smartest person in a room, find another room.

THE INSTRUCTOR TRAP | 23

Move and Think

Thursday was my return to teaching Systema after the birth of my daughter Petra. Time away always makes me think long and hard about both Systema and how I can best help my students improve *their* Systema.

I get a good laugh at what has become the standard Systema talk, e.g. "breathe", "relax" or "move." Student Steve Osborn knows I take piano lessons, so he is fond of saying, "yeah, and all you have to do is hit the right keys at the right time." See, this stuff is much easier said than done, and just because you can *say* it doesn't mean you can *do* it. Breathe, relax and move are correct principles, but sometimes students need a bit more direction to get them to breathe, relax and move correctly.

One glaring challenge most students have is rooting, not moving. "Move" doesn't always work as a teaching device, so while I was away I came up with an obvious solution — so obvious I've never seen anyone else ever teach it.

So I experimented in class to see if I could overcome this rooting/non-moving issue. I created a new rule for the *pervade =*

class: **you cannot stop moving until class is over**. We were all to keep in motion for an hour and thirty minutes, no matter what. They needed to move when I explained something, when they switched turns or switched partners, when they went to get a weapon or when they were knocked down. No stopping, ever.

Result? At only one point in class did anyone root...and he was just taking a break while I explained something. Tyler Scott even commented after our class, *"It just felt unnatural not to move."*

Mission Accomplished!

People think Vladimir just "is" this great martial artist. The truth is that he constantly improves and <u>thinks</u> about better ways to teach and do Systema. Years ago, around 2002, I was on the phone with him talking about teaching. He told me how whatever movement he shows he tries to do it in every way he can imagine, under every circumstance and with every body part. One of my Kenpo teachers called this thought process "cross-referencing" the move so that it <u>pervades</u> everything you do. Vladimir also talked to me about different ways to teach the same idea.

In addition to *"<u>not stopping</u>,"* I also instructed the students to *"<u>move and think</u>."*

I decided to come at this rooting problem from another angle. Students always find it easier to keep moving when they are already moving – the Law of Inertia – a body in motion tends to stay in motion. In addition, students always stop moving when they think they've recalled and executed a technique, which naturally has a beginning and an end.

It is cliché to say, *"Stop and think,"* because you stop

MOVE AND THINK | 25

moving, stand there and think of an answer to your problem and only then do you start moving again. This is all-too-common (and how it became cliché).

In Systema I say, *"Move and think,"* because you have to keep moving and allow your conscious mind to catch up to your natural movements. Putting everyone in constant movement for an extended period of time denied the students the luxury of judging or critiquing their movements. They just kept moving and trying, free from the paralysis of analysis. After about 30 minutes, students began to be able to meld their actions with their thoughts and performed beautifully.

To this day, students ask me, *"When will we do another one of those constant movement classes"?*

Yes You Can Watch, But Get on the Mat

Before I became a Systema Instructor, I was like most people new to the art. I had years of both previous training and pre-conceived notions of what martial arts are supposed to look like. Luckily, my training history along with my own insights allowed me to appreciate Systema. Other people who see Systema for the first time are not so fortunate. Here are three reasons you need to take a class to begin to understand Systema:

#1 Sitting there watching people do breathing exercises and calisthenics is boring. The students doing the exercises are challenging their bodies, creating a feeling of power and raising their energy. You cannot relate to this sitting there and watching.

#2 You may not see what you are expecting to see in class. Each class is unique, with a different area of focus, and is taught for those specific students who are there that day. If you are not in the class, then the work may not address your particular concerns. Perhaps you wanted to see groundwork while the class is doing stand-up work. Therefore, you dismiss the whole art based on one class, one that just happened to focus on stand-up work.

#3 Systema creates lots of "head-scratching moments" for people who watch it. A guy came to class once and we were doing some simple, subtle takedown work. I demonstrated and then had him try it with Brian. This guy followed my direction and Brian was losing his balance and falling down. So he asked me, *"is he just falling down or am I making him"?* I told him to let Brian try it on him.

So he attacked Brian and, as he was falling with that what-the-heck-is-happening look in his eyes, I smiled, looked down at him and said, *"Are you just falling down"?* He got it and laughed right back. Because he had it done to him and felt the effectiveness, he kept training. To someone sitting on the other side of the glass watching, this may look rather odd. However, feeling is believing.

So watch and see if you want, but get on the mat and feel it before you make any judgment — that is a true eye-opening and sometimes eye-closing, experience.

Newbies

One of the distinctions between Systema classes and other martial arts classes is that beginners and advanced students train together. Classes are very democratic. This is good because beginners can teach advanced students just as much, if not more, than the advanced students can teach beginners. Everyone learns from everyone else because every interaction with another person can teach you about tension, relaxation and how different bodies move. The tension, improper breathing and lack of movement that characterizes the beginning student serve as constant reminders to more advanced students to maintain self-control and remember the principles.

The challenge for the Systema beginner is that while learning the current topic, he may not know some of the fundamentals of Systema that other students take for granted. For example, in Systema students fall a lot, and everyone should learn how to fall and roll without getting hurt. Of course, every class cannot be about just the basics because a new student is in class otherwise long-time students would not learn anything new or take their skills to a higher level.

Here is a bare minimum of what a new student should know:

- *How to fall and roll without getting hurt.*
- *How to do basic Systema exercises.*
- *The structure of a Systema class.*

This is why I created a mini Quick-Start Video for my new Systema students in order to prepare them for their first class. You can check out our YouTube Channel, SystemaColorado.

In case you're wondering where this idea came from, it was from a new student. She jumped right into class — as do all new students — and after a few sessions she requested a class on how to fall and roll properly. This was a legitimate request and gave me this great idea. After all, the more I can prepare a beginner for class, the more time we can devote to advanced training in class. Finally, most of this foundational work can be done alone at home.

Four Types of Systema Students

There are four types of Systema students. Which one are you?

1) The "No Previous Experience" Student
2) The "Convert" Student
3) The "Improve My Original Art" Student
4) The "Bruce Lee-Mindset" Student

Let's take a look at each type of student:

1) The "No Previous Experience" Student

The "No Previous Experience" student is just that, a person who has not studied any martial art before stumbling onto Systema.

The advantage the "NPE" student has is that he hasn't ingrained bad habits of over-tensing, improper breathing, rooting and getting locked into a specific technique.

The disadvantage that the "NPE" student has is that he has no background knowledge of self-defense movements. If Systema is the martial art you've forgotten...well, first you have to have something to forget! This does not apply to the NPE Student. He needs *some* technique in his arsenal to then dissolve into his movements.

2) The "Convert" Student

The Convert Student does have previous martial art experience. He has abandoned his previous training and dived whole-heartedly into Systema. The Convert Student is the most common Systema student, particularly in places where Systema is totally new.

The advantage the Convert student has is that he may have months and usually years of background knowledge. When he finally finds Systema, it's easy for him to just not think about a particular technique he's done hundreds, if not thousands of times, and "let it happen." Systema can supercharge his years of acquired skills!

The disadvantage that the Convert student has is his previous training. He usually has bad habits like rooting, poor footwork, bad posture, holding his breath or not breathing at all and of course tension. Fortunately, these bad habits can be corrected in a relatively short period of time.

3) The "Improve My Original Art" Student

The "Improve My Original Art" Student just wants to cross-train in Systema a little bit. He might want to pick up some cool knife disarms, handgun defense or unique escapes from holds. His goal is to integrate these moves into his "main" martial art.

The advantage to the "Improve My Original Art" student is he can learn so many other moves, scenarios and training methods that will make *any* Art more effective. The IMOA student usually comes to Systema for this "secret knowledge" and then returns to his Original Art as a conquering hero. The ego-inflation here is measurable and palpable. Systema is his secret weapon to gain an advantage over his peers who are doing the same old same old. Just a drop of Systema skyrockets his respective skill in comparison to others in his original art. The beauty is that he can be fair at Systema but a "superstar" going back to his original art.

The disadvantage the IMOA student has is self-delusion. He becomes a big fish in a little pond while knowing there is a much larger ocean of potential knowledge that he is not tapping into. He goes to the ocean with a teaspoon thinking that's all there is.

4) The "Bruce Lee-Mindset" Student

The "Bruce Lee-Mindset" student has "no way as his way." He has no loyalty to any martial system. His goal is to absorb what is useful and to discard what is useless.

The advantage of the BLM student is he has no hang-ups, no master telling him what to do or not to do. He is free to learn any martial art idea that will make him a better martial artist. His loyalty is to himself, not to any art. This is a powerful mindset but...

The disadvantage of the BLM student is the "jack of all trades, master of none" trap. The danger of not listening to a teacher or persisting in developing key skills can keep the BLM student just average in many martial arts.

So Which Student Are You? Or, Which Type *Should* You Be?

If you are new, there is nothing you can do about that. Get on with your Systema training. However, you must be taught the correct martial arts attacks such as locks, chokes, takedowns, knife attacks, etc. If you are lucky enough to have a teacher who knows and can teach these skills to you then it is all the better. If your teacher doesn't, or doesn't know himself, the danger is you may not learn how to defend against realistic attacks.

If you are a convert student — as most people are — don't forget your old art, just stop trying to force techniques into a specific situation. You may be much more likely to just stop thinking and allow your body to react if you have had solid, realistic training prior to Systema.

If you are the Improve My Original Art Student...well... you're missing the point. I have nothing else for you.

As for the Bruce Lee Mindset Student, I believe this is your eventual mindset destination. At some point in your training, you will believe that Systema is the be-all, end-all (which it could be). But, if you interact with enough high-level martial artists from the best systems you will come to the realization that they have much to offer.

Sometimes a little technique will elevate your skills. For example, Filipinos are masters at short stick fighting. Why reinvent the wheel? Just a short time with their art, coupled with Systema will take your skill to new levels. Likewise, BJJ/Sambo/Catch Wrestling have an entire world of training to offer you. Why not spend a bit of time at least learning the basics and then combining it with your Systema principles? The difference is obvious.

Why People Quit

"Face your fear, and watch it disappear"

I've often thought of taping every class and having someone transcribe all the conversation, including the end circle, because there's much wisdom to be shared there.

Here's a recap of Thursday's end circle:

Lately, our topic has been "up close and personal" knife work. I've spent a lot of time showing students the best, hardest-to-defend ways to attack with a knife. This includes not only the ability to use a knife, but so everyone's defenses would be ready for these types of attacks. Naturally this entails stabbing each other, which elicits some deep-seating emotions in students.

As nonchalant as we can be with knives — because we are used to training with them — to a new student the whole topic can be scary, threatening and repulsive. It's just not normal to stab people (a good thing for society). If you're teaching the military or LEO's then there is already an acceptance and appreciation for weapons work. Psychologically, these types of students are more mentally and emotionally prepared for this work than civilians are.

This isn't a knife-fighting chapter; it's just that working with knives often highlights one of the main reasons people quit Systema — **being uncomfortable.**

Having taught Systema for over a decade, I've observed this phenomenon time and again. I've written about it, I tell people about it in class and I warn people about it in a letter I send to prospective students.

So what makes people uncomfortable in Systema Class? The act of having to face what makes them uncomfortable or scares them regardless of what element of training it might be. (duh)

In the knife work example, a student who is uncomfortable with this work might just avoid it altogether. The "negative" emotions — fear, the heebie-jeebies — pop up and the easiest way to dispel them is not come to class. No class, no bad feelings. They quit.

This is the coward's way out. But it is all too common (normal).

The frustrating part of this dynamic for Systema teachers is **we know that facing discomfort and fear head-on and overcoming it is a major benefit of Systema training.** If there were one lesson I'd want students to take from class, it would be this.

Oddly enough, students who do stay come up to me and say things like, *"this (kind of situation) freaks me out. Can we work on this?"* That's courage and emotional maturity.

Take a few minutes and delve into what "freaks you out." Is it:

- knives,
- sticks,
- whips,
- punches,
- joint locks
- being held down
- being choked?

Whatever it is, capture it, write it down and lay it bare for you to see and put into a healthy perspective. When you have the chance, come to class and consciously, purposefully, address your fear. You will see your fear and discomfort disappear, often in one class.

The Kettlebell Controversy

Ok, here's a Hot Topic that gets tossed around, well, like a kettlebell, in Systema Circles everywhere. The Controversy? ***Should You Use Kettlebells as part of your Systema Training?*** Before I answer this, let me say that I teach a Kettlebell Class right before my Systema classes. Most of these students are NOT Systemists, but some are.

On the NO side...both Mikhail and Vladimir believe that you don't need kettlebells (or weight training) for Systema and recommend other exercises and methods to improve your Systema.

On the YES side...are students and teachers who believe that training with kettlebells is beneficial to their Systema training.

Take a look at the benefits of kettlebell training and IF you need them for Systema, and to what degree.

> #1 Kettlebells are great for weight-loss. There is no denying this. If you are trying to shed pounds, they are great.

#2 Kettlebells are a simple way to work out on your own.
#3 Kettlebells can help reinforce proper body alignment
#4 Kettlebells can be used to strengthen movements needed in Systema, like one-leg squats.
#5 Kettlebells can teach you how to use only the tension you need under resistance and how to work with it.
#6 Kettlebells are fun and anything that gets you moving is better than lying on the couch.
#7 Kettlebells can really fatigue you and make you feel "heavy"

OK, those are the Basic Pro's for using kettlebells for Systema. Now for the flip-side...

#1 Kettlebells tend to make you stiff (just look at the average girevik)...unless you make a conscious effort to keep yourself loose. They create the unconscious Habit of Tensing — bad for Systema.
#2 Kettlebell training tends to teach your how to root, grip the floor and keep you in one spot. This is definitely another bad habit for Systema.
#3 Kettlebell breathing as commonly taught is totally incompatible with Systema. *"Power-Lifting" Breathing has next to nothing to do with Systema breathing. Just try to take a punch with kettlebell-breathing!*
#4 Kettlebell training doesn't cover all the "movement dynamics" needed in Systema. The types of motion and positions in Systema just cannot be addressed with heavy weights.

This leads to the next question...Can any benefits of kettlebells for Systema be had through other training methods?

- **Weight-Loss?** Definitely you can do this without kettlebells.
- **Working out on your own?** Don't need kettlebells.
- **Body Alignment?** Don't need kettlebells.
- **Strengthening Systema moves?** Don't need kettlebells.
- **Learning to work with resistance, and with little tension?** Don't need kettlebells.
- **Making you feel heavy?** Don't need kettlebells.

(Side note: The WarriorFit System I created covers all of this — without kettlebells!)

Clearly Mikhail and Vladimir are correct...that you don't need kettlebells to improve your Systema...and in fact, there are some big negatives that can adversely affect your Systema performance, *if* left unchecked.

It boils down to this.

What is your Primary Goal? If it is to improve your Systema, then **you should be doing the exercises that most directly improve your Systema.**

How much time do you have to devote to training? If you are limited, then hard-core Systema exercises ONLY. If you have more time, then add some kettlebell training, but be sure to compensate for the potential negatives.

What do you like and what amount of kettlebell training would you like to add to your regimen? My students who like KB's, love them. Fantastic. And, as I said, some of my KB students go right into Systema class and work on Systema after KB training and they report that that helps them in Systema. They're lucky.

One Last Thing:

In my own experience I can say that I like KB's and use them sparingly, definitely as a supplement, and not too much.

I've had a difficult time putting it into words but on a deep level I believe Mikhail...when it comes to KB's and mastering Systema. There's a difference in how I feel my body — its interconnectedness and unity — in Systema that I don't get with kettlebells. I feel like I "have to get that feeling back after I've done lots of kettlebelling."

This is why I'm stressing "kettlebells for Systema" and not just "generic kettlebell training". Outside of Systema, I recommend kettlebells for most everyone, no doubt.

The Kettlebell Controversy – Part 2

Considering the response I got from the last article, people have some, shall we say "strong views" on kettlebell training, both for and against. The Controversy Continues...***Should You Use Kettlebells as part of your Systema Training?***

You know I hate the word "should" (and its corollary "should not"). So, my short answer to everyone here is **if you like it, do it,** along with my slightly less-short answer, whatever gets you moving and exercising is better than reclining in your La-Z-Boy.

Ok, so you've decided to "Kettlebell It." The question now becomes, WHAT exercises should you do and how should you do them? Let's look at the most common Kettlebell exercise:

The Swing/Snatch As you know these exercises require that you hinge at your hips and bend forward — in Systema what we refer to as "breaking your structure." *The Danger?* It is through hundreds of repetitions ingraining the habit of bending over and breaking your own structure.

There are two main schools of thought, or methods, of kettlebell training popular in the U.S.

The RKC (Russian Kettlebell Club), also called "Hardstyle," focuses on maximum muscle tension and breathing methods akin to hard style martial arts.

The AKC/WKC (American/World Kettlebell Club) focuses on proper body alignment, efficiency and Systema-like breathing.

The RKC method, now called "Hard style," has you bend your knees and hips while keeping your head looking straight ahead as you perform the swing.

The AKC method hip-hinges with a slight knee-bend. It keeps your entire spine straight and aligned, with your head following the bell during the swing. (There are other differences that are not pertinent here.)

For Systema, I recommend the AKC style because you can think of the swing as a vertical Systema Sit-Up. The principles of the AKC also align better with Systema ideas of relaxation, breathing and body alignment.

Here's just one good exercise you can do with kettlebells. Perform Systema-type squats with the kettlebells to ingrain proper form for combat. Over the years I routinely have had students hold a weight out in front of them to help their squat form, especially if they can't put their heels on the floor. Who knew someone would come along and give it a super-cool name? So do this Goblet Squat, or Front Squat, with the Bells in the Clean Position.

250 lb. Man Knocked Down with No Physical Contact

I was watching the Minnesota Vikings play the Dallas Cowboys. On a recent play, Brett Favre was about to be sacked by a charging DeMarcus Ware, who came in unblocked from the right as Favre was looking left.

Just as he was about to be sacked, Favre dropped his shoulder and fell to the ground. Ware went flying over him just as his arms were about to encircle Favre. Favre's timing was perfect, impeccable and driven by self-preservation against an all-out assault.

Contrast this with a video clip of the Yellow Bamboo System martial artist who attempts the same, ducking strategy against a charging BBJ stylist. As he ducks, he is mounted and choked out by the grappler. This clip has garnered thousands of chuckles across cyberspace. Poor guy.

So what's the difference? A lot actually.

Like most things, context is the key.

In the Yellow Bamboo example, it was a one-on-one, head-to-head confrontation. The "attacker" *knew* and was ready to anticipate, and respond to the defender's movement, whatever it may have been. This was set-up in the fight. *"You attack and I 'will do something' to defend..."* He knew the defender was ready for him and was waiting for his first counter-move so he could adjust. The BJJ attacker knew his defender was going to do <u>something</u> so he was looking for that something so he could counter it. And he did. I'd have done the same thing.

In the earlier example, Ware attacked with total confidence and commitment because he knew he had Favre *"dead to rights."* He had a solid target that apparently wasn't ready for his attack. He thought he had him and just knew he was going to level Favre. He didn't.

I love football because of its unabashed physicality. I especially love watching those great players, like the late Walter Payton of Chicago Bears fame, who had the rare skill of being able to make tacklers miss at will. *"They almost had him,"* just before ending up on the turf with Payton running for a touchdown.

So, the strategy to get the heck out of the way by ducking is a sound one, but it takes lots of practice to develop the correct sensitivity and timing. **And the Yellow Bamboo guy should have had some other skills to employ when his "technique" didn't work. Football players, and good martial artists, do.**

Note: I'm not sure how much DeMarcus Ware weighs...

I Know Systema Works Because I'm Doing It Wrong

The End Circle at the close of Systema class yields some insightful one-liners from students. The title quote, "I know Systema works because I am doing it wrong," is a paraphrase of a comment routinely given by student Andrew Walton. It is one of my favorite quotes and here is how it originated.

I would demonstrate a certain principle and show some work followed by the class practicing, a typical Systema class. Andrew liked to have me do the work to him because he is a very physical learner. Once he felt it, he would understand it and then continue to practice.

As sure as day, Andrew wouldn't be able to make anything I showed work on his partner and get frustrated. As class went on he would invariably do the work exactly as he had it explained and demonstrated to him and he would send his partner flying to the ground.

I like Andrew's observation because it makes a profound distinction in training. One, he watched me do the work successfully on someone, seeing how it is done. Two, he would see me do the work successfully on his partner, so he knew it would work on his partner. Up to this point Andrew could think that his partners are "just letting me do the work." But then, three, he would feel me successfully do the work on him, so there is no doubt that Systema works on him. Here is the distinction. Andrew sees and feels the work done correctly so he knows I can do it. Now it is only a question of whether he could do it also.

As Andrew looked at his own training, he realized that there was nothing different about his training partner. I could do the work on him, Andrew failed to do the work, and then, with some practice, he also had a degree of success. All that changed was *how* Andrew did the work himself.

When he began to breathe, relax, keep Form and move, everything started working for him. These are the basic Systema principles and when he violated them nothing worked for him — he was doing it wrong. Whenever he corrected himself and applied the Systema principles, everything worked. Hence his conclusion, Systema works because he was doing it wrong.

It doesn't get any clearer than that.

Ever Get That Funny Feeling?

Recently I've had "that funny feeling" on three separate occasions — where I ran into someone whom I couldn't quite place. I ran into the Context Problem. I wasn't in the place where I met any of these three so I couldn't put their faces into the correct context to recall who they were.

I know you've been there too.

You run into a person and keep thinking, *"I know that person from SOMEwhere, but where?"* This is a dreadful state of mind because, first of all, when it happens, you don't know whether it's a positive or negative relationship. Is it a good thing to run into this person or not? Or would you rather not have this person see you? You've been caught off-guard and have yet to regain your bearings.

Second, you flip through your mental rolodex trying to match the face with some memory, any fragment of a memory that you can reconstruct. *(Yes, reconstruct. Don't get me started on the New Age claptrap that we all have some perfect memory, like taking a picture. Brain research has proven that memories are stored all over your brain and reconstructed.)*

That leads to the next issue, relating the face to the name. We always remember faces and names not so much, lending a bit more to the awkwardness of your chance encounter. So what do you do? You go with the flow, hoping that something the person says will trigger your recall.

Then comes the face-saving move, the person recognizes you and says, *"Hi, it's (ME),"* giving you his or her name. The name releases the mnemonic floodgate allowing you to recall the context and smoothly continue the conversation like a normal person.

I wouldn't even mention this, but like I said, I found myself in this socially awkward situation three times in the past few weeks. I've gotten on familiar terms with that funny feeling lately, and it got me to thinking about my Systema students because, **isn't that funny feeling what students go through in every class, especially new students?**

First, comes the sudden or surprise attack (because in Systema we don't tell the person how we are going to attack) that takes you off your guard. Your brain yells, *"Do something, now!" "But what?"* you ask. Here's where new students get stuck, stop, turn to me and say, *"I don't know what to do."*

With a little training, new students figure out that going anywhere is better than where they are now, so they move. This may not be the complete solution, but it's a good start. Your brain is still searching for an answer, like trying to recall a name.

As the attacker continues, and you continue to move, seemingly from out of nowhere comes the answer. You sense your opportunity, act and the attacker is subdued. And all is right in the world, for now.

Walking Through Fog

Getting past that funny feeling and stumbling upon a solution, be it a name or an effective defense means that you have to do just that, stumble. You must move.

Imagine that you are out walking in your neighborhood and a thick fog descends all around you. You want to get home, and generally know the way home but you are unsure, hence a bit apprehensive, of where to step to next. You can only see a step or two in front of you before the fog obscures your field of vision.

A funny thing happens when you take a step – you see the next step or two in front of you. Continue this and eventually you will find your way home, even though you could never have found the way standing in one place, standing still. When you take a step toward the answer, it takes a step toward you.

Elsewhere, I spoke about people quitting because they feel uncomfortable. Well, "that funny feeling" is an extension of that discomfort. When you realize and accept that your answers come out of your movement you will find more answers.

In the immortal words of Indiana Jones — responding to the question, *"what are you going to do now?"* — *"I don't know, I'm making it up as I go."*

What about Resistance?

If you practice Systema for any length of time you will invariably run into the *"Would that work against someone who resists?"* question or its variant pronouncement, *"that wouldn't work against someone who resists!"* Here's a quick explanation to keep you from foaming at the mouth while wanting to scream, *"It does too, and it works even better when you resist."*

A core Systema principle is to relax while under attack, both mentally and physically, so you can respond most effectively and efficiently (minimum force, maximum effect). Students practice an entire battery of drills and exercises to learn how to use only the necessary and sufficient amount of tension to dispatch attackers. One misunderstanding is that people think these drills represent self-defense. In reality, they only constitute one part of self-defense training.

One common, detrimental side-effect of this *"over-relaxed, flaccid,"* training is that students forget to resist when they are the attacker in training. This type of asymmetrical training — where the attacker throws one attack, then lets the defender successfully do whatever he wants — gives rise to the reasonable objection, *"would that work if I resisted (kept attacking and countering)?"*

Sadly, I've seen the answer to this question all too many times...and the answer was, for many practitioners, no it wouldn't work. Don't let this be you.

Systema is not alone in facing this criticism. Any martial art that lacks continuous, free-form exchange between combatants is open to this argument. Arts like Kali, Judo and Jiu-jitsu, boxing and wrestling that use their techniques in dynamic free-form sparring situations are better-equipped to deal with the uncertainty and *"all plans change upon contact"* nature of fighting than arts, and martial artists, that don't.

The fact is that Systema **does** contain free-form elements or at least it should. Training at Systema Colorado includes a ton of this training. The problem is that students and instructors sometimes forget that just becoming a noodle is not the point of self-defense it is a means of only using sufficient tension. Being able to work against a persistent, intelligent, resistant and resistive attacker is the ultimate skill to master, not working against someone who'll just take a dive no matter what you do.

To be fair, the best Systemists have trained for and against intelligent attackers and they still make it look easy. I watch closely when someone wanted to go at it with Mikhail. I watch for their follow-up attacks and adjustments to his movements. Mikhail is responding to all of their moves and counters at an almost imperceptible level, subduing them with ease. I can see the back and forth happening where someone new to Systema would totally overlook it.

Yet, watch the older tapes of him and you will see him using a bit more tension because he was not yet the consummate master that he is now after years of this type of training.

The short answer to the resistance question is highly-skilled Systemists, like highly-skilled grapplers continuously use the attacker's tension and movement against him through high-level sensitivity and endless repetitions of the scenarios.

5 Simple Steps to Train against Resistance

How do you get to this point other than practice? Well, it's <u>how</u> you practice.

1) Once you hit the milestone of being able to relax while under attack,
2) Your next goal is to use minimum necessary force in your counter-attacks.
3) Then, you should practice learning to stay relaxed against faster and faster attacks, up to full-speed.
4) Now, you can work against a "dumb" resisting attacker, someone who is stiff and won't move when you try to move his body. Your goal at this stage is to stay relaxed when he is tense so you don't get frustrated, amped up and just push harder. This stage trips up many Systemists because they become accustomed to the other person yielding and it's a shock when he doesn't. I've even seen instructors stop and complain that the person is too tense because they *"couldn't work."* This is a cover-up of not being able to work against tension.

5) Finally, move on to the attacker resisting and countering your movements in a true free-form exchange — Systema sparring. Again, start slowly and move to full-speed.

If you can do all of the above, then you can honestly, affirmatively answer The Resistance Question the best way — *physically*.

So Striking Is Love, Huh?

When I began martial arts training and even before I began martial arts training, I was astute enough to know that being hit wasn't much fun — from first-hand experience. That's exactly why I started learning martial arts in the first place, because getting hit hurt and was not the kind of thing I trolled the streets as a kid asking people to help me out with. I was usually running in the opposite direction.

The logic was sound. If strikes hurt me, they'd sure hurt the bullies too. Learning how to strike — and avoiding getting struck — made sense. It still makes sense, on the surface.

Enter Systema. A bunch of guys standing around letting their instructor punch them until they puke. Oh, and it is love. What gives?

I started writing an answer, then put this aside because this is a broad and deep topic that is almost too much for one little chapter. I'll try to get to the main discussion I had about "striking=love" that prompted me to put fingers to keyboard.

Why would you stand there and let someone cause you

intense physical pain and think it was because the person loved you?

Outside of Systema, if you said this to someone they might recommend a good therapist. Battered wives sometimes need their abusive husbands to hit them because they learn to equate the beatings with attention and affection. I've even had students who thought I didn't like them if I didn't punch them. Somehow this strikes me as a tad dysfunctional, but I could be wrong.

Why didn't I want to be hit during my youth? Because of the pain I knew striking caused — from direct experience.

I recently saw an episode of Human Impossible by National Geographic that sheds some light into the "dynamics of striking." One portion of the episode featured a woman who had hooks inserted under the skin of her upper back and swung around the room by the chains. She reported that it initially hurt to put the hooks in, but then she said that the experience became intensely enjoyable and even exhilarating. However...after about 10 minutes the pain returned to the point of becoming unbearable. Here's the scientific explanation:

In response to the pain, her body released its load of endorphins to counteract the pain. This accounted for her feelings of ecstasy. Then, after about 10 minutes her endorphin supply depleted itself. This led back to the considerable pain.

Wow! So, the body reacts to the pain of being struck with its own homemade morphine, killing the pain and making you feel great so you can go on and survive the encounter.

An interesting implication is that it is not the strike so much as it is your body's physiological response to the strike. Your response is the benefit.

I remember back to sparring "pre-Systema" and having the same feelings of elation and the sparring-high from all the give and take of strikes, regardless of the intention of the other person. I was having fun myself and welcomed the contact.

Watch someone being struck by a deep Systema punch. Does the contorted grimace look like love to you? It's only what the body does to save itself that makes you feel better.

So is that love or are we all just endorphin junkies?

Further Russian Striking Experiments

Russian scientists, headed by biologist Sergei Speransky, actually ran experiments on the curative powers of a good caning on the buttocks. They concluded that caning releases endorphins that make people feel good, reduce appetite and even boosts their immune systems. They also claim the euphoria lifts depression and addiction.

They now charge over $100 per session for caning therapy. According to Dr Marina Chuhrova, who regularly canes about 10 patients, *"At first they didn't like it, but when they started to feel the benefits they kept asking for more."*

Dr. Speransky believes that caning is more effective than other, less painful methods such as through food, exercise or bodywork and advocates combining all these methods for the best results, *"that way you can get a maximum dose of endorphins."*

So Striking Is Love, Huh? Part 2

I was going to write about a topic near and dear to my heart, but I figured I'd get back to this whole "Striking is Love" thing first.

As I talked about last time, standing there and letting someone hit you is not normal...and being afraid of being hit and the accompanying pain is normal. I asked Vladimir what the hardest part of Systema was for him when he was learning and he said *"taking strikes, because I was so skinny."* Vladimir's answer should give you some insight on striking.

I will not address this entire list today, but here are **10 Aspects of Striking to Consider** before you start indiscriminately start wailing on people:

- It hurts
- Fear of being hurt
- Emotional experiences of prior abuse resurfacing
- Pre-existing conditions, e.g. having tachycardia or previous injury
- Memories of being hit hard or hurt by the striker previously

- Fear of appearing weak in front of others if you show pain.
- Mistrust, leading to fear and tension, toward the person striking you, or knowing the striker has no idea what he's doing.
- The misguided notion that *any* pain or injury is actually in the best interests of the person being hit
- Ego of the striker, wanting to prove how hard he can hit you.
- Finally, the idea that the striking is "medicine," how it should be dispensed and by whom.

I came back from a seminar years ago in Florida where we were all hit repeatedly with an Escrima stick. Yes, it was a painful experience that I would not volunteer to go through again on a regular basis, but I survived and admittedly felt like I could take any hit and be OK.

The after-effects were pretty major. My entire abdomen was bruised for at least a week, if not more. It looked like I spilled grape juice all over my stomach. It did help me keep my Form because I couldn't bend. :)

A few days later, I happened to see my sister, a nurse, who about fainted when she saw my "souvenir." I got the lecture about hematoma, blood clotting and internal damage, etc. After I got over my macho "but I did it" phase, I thought a bit deeper into what she was telling me, that striking could cause major short-term or long-term damage.

I'm going to jump to #10 — the idea that striking is somehow medicine. Let's look at other "doctors" who dispense medicine for a comparison.

Doctors have to be licensed and go through the appropriate training to be considered qualified to dispense medicine. You can't just open a medical practice and start prescribing drugs to people. So, I'd be leery of just any guy at a seminar punching me willy-nilly, even knowing that I can deal with punches. That's natural. Fear of idiots, especially with a little power and in numbers, is high on my list.

Before prescribing any medicine doctors do an evaluation of the patient and his history. I have a student with tachycardia, an abnormally rapid heart rate, so punching him in the chest over and over is out of the question — and has nothing to do with "being strong." I don't feel like having a dead guy on my mat. Do you ask your partner if there's anything out of the ordinary, or that you should know about before you hit him?

Doctors know what the medicine they prescribe does to people. Does the guy hitting you? Does the strike do exactly what he expects, or is he just throwing it and waiting to see what might happen? If you don't know — find a qualified instructor.

Doctors have your best interest at heart — they are trying to help you. I've seen all too many chuckleheads punching a guy standing there as hard as they can with zero regard for him, striking out of anger and ego. It is even worse when they get mad when the other person hits them. This is only made worse when the person can hit hard (I've been on the receiving end of this several times and this could hardly be called anything close to "love.")

I'll close with this quick example. It's about an instructor, drunk with power, going around punching people saying, *"I'm healing people, I'm healing people..."* not being aware that he broke someone's sternum, broke another student's rib and injured a few others with his "healing." Healing like that, I don't need. Sigh.

Striking IS awesome, fun and essential to self-defense training. Striking just has to be approached the right way by someone competent and whom you trust.

Striking Is Love, Part 3

I've heard people say that, not only is striking love, but that every strike heals you. Out came my contrarian nature...

The first time Mikhail punched me was like nothing I'd ever felt before. I'd been punched many times in the solar plexus but not like that. This was well before Russians knew how to translate into English the sage advice, *"don't bend over when struck."*

It felt like I put my finger in an electric socket. The strike was something other than pain. I felt like my body was experiencing a power surge or an energy overload. I started sweating from my palms and feet, and I felt like my head was going to burst. It felt like I was exploding from the solar plexus to my extremities.

I had to sit down and put my head down. Vladimir noticed me sitting there. He quickly came over to me and pulled the energy out of my head to restore me to normal. I told him what I described here and he just smiled and nodded in agreement.

That one strike was a game-changer. I had to learn how to

understand what happened, to be able to survive it and how to strike like that myself.

Mikhail's strike was a healing strike; it led me on the path of developing internal strength and I am grateful for it. He also directly made me aware of the very real connection between mind, thoughts and body. The Systema striking method is unequaled for dissipating fear and is an invaluable gift for martial artists.

The idea that <u>every</u> strike heals you is ludicrous on the face of it. I know of practitioners who have had ribs broken, sterna broken and muscles torn from being hit by these "healing strikes." Simply defining everything as healthy doesn't make it so. Perhaps the strikes are healing in the sense, *"now that you are broken, your body has to heal what the strike just broke."*

The danger of this rationalization is that it removes responsibility from the striker. *"Oh, I broke your jaw? You must have needed a healing."* This mentality frees people to indiscriminately hurt people when they define hurting as healing. Yes, in every hardship there is an opportunity for growth but hardship and pain do not necessarily create growth, and can even make things worse.

Nietzsche believed," *What does not destroy me, makes me stronger."* but sometimes, *"what does not destroy me, makes me weak enough for something else to finish the job."*

If you don't trust 'em, don't let 'em hit you.

Punch Like a Prius

You may have seen the big news recently, that Toyota, the World's #1 Automobile Manufacturer is having some significant safety issues with its cars.

First, due to design flaws, their floor mats are getting in the way of their brakes.

Then, much worse, the brakes on their Prius models were discovered to, how shall we say, not work!

So there you are, accelerating along in your enviro-mobile when you see a gas-guzzling SUV. You try to hit the brakes — no brakes — and POW! You are out of the gene pool. Maybe that's why it's so earth-friendly — with so many Priuses out there, soon there'll be fewer people driving.

It gives a whole new meaning to their slogan, *"moving forward" (because you can't stop)*.

Oh yeah, Systema. So there I was, teaching a striking class on Saturday when I noticed a student tensing his whole shoulder girdle every time he threw a punch. It was just killing his power.

You know, most martial arts teach just that, *"tense on*

impact." After a decade-plus of Systema, I'm sure the guy who wrote this gem of wisdom down carelessly omitted the key phrase, *"just your fist,"* leading generations of martial artists to tense their entire bodies when they punch.

I began a lengthy explanation of how tension of your "stopper muscles" keeps your power from transferring into the target and how your fist should be solid...yadda, yadda... when it hit me — *some (most) times simple is best.*

So I asked the class if they'd heard about Toyota. They had. To which I responded, **"Punch Like a Prius — No Brakes."**

After the laughter died down everyone immediately began punching harder and deeper.

Thanks Toyota.

The Reality of the Short Stick

What can I say? Saturday's Weapons Day Workshop rocked. I'm continually amazed at Al McLuckie's stick progressions and teaching methodology to get Systema students working with short, one-handed sticks in one day.

I also appreciated his *"Stick Reality"* demonstration. To recap, he had Hadi Ali and Scott Crawford strike each other in the body with sticks, each one waving off the fairly deep strikes.

Next, he asked them to perform the same drill, but this time targeting only bones, the skull, clavicle elbow, knee, shins, hand, etc. He said to do this only as hard and fast as they think they could take. Needless to say, they did this drill <u>slowly</u> and <u>lightly</u>.

Then, Al walked over to a heavy bag with a very heavy wooden stick and struck it full-speed, full-force. He hit the bag with multiple strikes in a fraction of a second, from all different angles. He said, *"Now this is how a trained stick fighter would attack you."*

The contrast between that strike and how Hadi and Scott

were working made his point loud and clear about the danger of a hard stick in the hands of a skilled practitioner. It was eye-opening for everyone in the room.

This is what decades of hard-core stick training, with over a decade and a half of Systema mechanics layering on top of it gets you. I see Al moving rapidly toward being able to use a short stick the way high-level Systemists use our hands, not just striking, but locking, breaking structure, with continuous control from any angle, range or use of the stick. Talk about the stick being *"an extension of his body."*

You know, I'd say that Al wields the stick like a master painter — which he is — wields a paint brush, but that'd be too easy in this case...

Fighting...with Sticks

It's been too long since fellow Senior Systema Instructor Martin Wheeler has visited Colorado, but fortunately Hollywood didn't keep him away this weekend. You know I'm not one for meticulously writing a review explaining every little drill Martin taught. That would be a particularly "un-Systema-like" review. Rather, I'll recap what Martin was trying to teach this weekend. What I can say is that everyone had short sticks in their hands the entire weekend. One day on the ground, the next standing.

Martin taught what he excels at, moving with an attacker and creating an effective response off the movement. The stick was just another tool he used to get the point across. Of course, there are specific things to know about working with or against a short stick and students learned this as well. The stick is a good teacher, it is unfeeling and unforgiving, forcing everyone to move correctly or get dinged. After all this time in Systema, it still amazes me how this simple concept of moving, then finding a way to effectively diffuse an attack works so well that even a student with zero martial art experience, like Todd Winkler, could come to the seminar and be putting guys on the ground in a matter of a few minutes with this training and exploring.

One key principle that Martin stressed with the stick, or any object, was that it is a tool and you are the weapon. People have a tendency to put their psyche into a weapon, in this case the stick, and completely forget that they have other tools and ways of fighting. In an instant, the stick may be disarmed, change possession or be rendered momentarily ineffectual. *"It's not fighting with sticks, it's fighting...with sticks."*

That pause makes all the difference in how you use a stick.

What, Just One Guy?

Vern Bevan commented after class that he'd never been in or seen a fight that was against just one guy. Many of us concurred that altercations we've been in or been witness to have been with multiple belligerents.

What is the point?

Well, we've been doing a good deal of innovative multiple/mass attack work in class lately in direct defiance of the *"conventional wisdom/drinking the kool-aid"* dogma that *"you can't beat more than one of you, so why try"* that is so prevalent in the Jiu-Jitsu/MMA world.

So...in even a relatively small group, such as our school, people say mass fighting is the norm...but "don't train to survive it" is the martial art zeitgeist?

That's plain stupid.

"Sorry, Mr. Home Invaders, I can only fight one at a time. Please wait your turn."

"Excuse me, Mr. Arrest Suspect, I can only get one of you under control at a time. Would you wait so I can arrest you later?"

"Boys, Gang-Rapists, I can only fend off one person at a time while I'm on the ground. So don't all jump me at once."

I don't think so.

If defending yourself from multiple attackers means that you will be seriously hurt, then your training should at least help you to become less-seriously hurt, if not just getting out alive or escaping to safety.

Given that mass/multiple attackers is a reality, training for anything less is irresponsible.

What, Just One Guy? Part 2

On the flipside of the *"you can't fight more than one guy"* argument is the view that you must only train BJJ/MMA to be any good as a martial artist. So, I find it fascinating that our own Aaron Trujillo went and, on a lark, entered a Jiu-Jitsu tournament this month, both no-gi and with-gi divisions.

In the with-gi division he made the Final-4, fighting several matches to get there. He got triangled when the other guy pulled the back of Aaron's gi-top over Aaron's own head. The ref even tried to help him get it off during the match. But except for that, Aaron was dominating the match. Sportsman-like, I don't know, but I guess it was legal. Lesson learned.

I give Aaron a ton of credit because he just started doing a very little bit of "gi-grappling" in the past month or so before the tournament. He was going against guys who only train for these things.

Aaron won 2nd place in the no-gi division, again fighting several matches to get there. I only saw a tape of his last fight, which he lost on points. Aaron was again poised throughout the fight and his opponent refused to go to the ground and stalled a lot. Aaron was on the offensive the whole time.

I mention this because, as I told Aaron, **none of those guys could even expect to walk into a Systema class and look like anything other than someone with no martial arts experience. Yet, he walked onto their playground and did just fine.** He reported that he was never out of breath, nervous, or felt like he was in over his head.

A true testament to his Systema training!

Bad Analogies

In an effort to understand Systema, people often fall back on analogies to give one another a better sense of the essence of Systema. All of these efforts are doomed to failure because, *"Systema cannot be explained, it can only be experienced."* Due to not being able to explain Systema, people naturally turn to what it is like, kind of. There are two very popular, yet woefully inadequate analogies people use in martial arts in general:

Bad Analogy #1: The Toolbox Analogy

The Toolbox analogy refers to the idea that techniques are like a carpenter's tools. The more tools you have in your toolbox the better off you are; you can do more because you have the tool for the job. This analogy is dangerous not only because of what it fails to address but also due to the type of training it fosters.

First, why might the Toolbox Analogy be helpful? At first, beginners do need examples of how they can move, escape and defend themselves. Specific work, movement or techniques do expand a beginner's knowledge base and are indeed helpful. The question becomes how many tools, or techniques, does one need and at what point is having too many techniques counterproductive. There is also the practical issue of how much *time* can you actually devote to practicing all the techniques that you have in your toolbox.

If you think having more tools is the answer to self-defense, you naturally become a technique collector. This type of student replaces the mindset of training with one of "having seen that." The Collector just wants to see enough different techniques so he can talk about them and show them off. He is like a gear-head who wants to show off all of his cool new tools to his neighbor.

The 80/20 Rule states that 80% of your success comes from 20% of your actions and that only 20% of your success comes from 80% of your actions — that all inputs do not yield the same results. The rule directly applies to adding more tools to your martial arts toolbox. The majority of techniques taught in martial arts schools are for such rare situations that time spent training in more common situations would be much better invested. Learning the "counter-to-the-counter-to-the-counter-to-the technique" sequence is training for something with slim odds of ever occurring outside the martial arts school.

I have heard the argument that if you don't memorize and collect the technique (tool) then it will be lost. The simple answer is then **let it be lost**. There are plenty of tools in museums that are no longer necessary or functional. Martial arts techniques are the same. Some things should be left behind as they are the product of a bygone age when perhaps they were needed, but no longer. Technique collecting begins to serve the martial art instead of serving the person.

I am sure that those of us with hundreds of tools have all had the experience of having to laboriously search to find a tool we need. Time wasted digging through your toolbox or garage (giant toolbox) can be frustrating. However, imagine struggling to find, recall and use your tool (technique) when someone suddenly attacks you.

More often than not people do not have the right tool with them when they need it anyway. I have had plenty of situations where I have had the right tool for what I needed but it was at home in my toolbox. I have learned to jury-rig, make do with what I had, or adapt other tools for the job like MacGyver who could do anything with duct tape and chewing gum. The whole appeal of the TV show was MacGyver's inventiveness and creativity, working with just a few tools.

Here is another major limitation of the Toolbox Analogy. A carpenter and I could have all the same tools in our toolboxes, yet he could build a house with them whereas I could not. First, there may be tools in my toolbox that I have no idea what they even are or how they work. Second, I may not have any experience with certain tools even though I may know how they are supposed to work. Just having and knowing your tools is not enough, you have to have the time and experience using them. We all know of techniques that we have learned but admit we would never even try because deep inside we know we could not make them work.

The Toolbox Analogy implies that you are not the answer to the attack, but rather you have to go outside of yourself to find, retrieve and use the tool to fix your problem. Yes, you do need a minimum knowledge base from which to work but technique collecting is not the answer. With the simple principles of Systema — breathing, relaxing, moving, and structure — you will create cooler and more effective techniques than you could ever memorize.

You are the weapon regardless of the tools you have.

Bad Analogies, Part 2

Bad Analogy #2: The Chess Match
People often compare martial arts to a game of chess, apparently because chess is seen as the premier game of strategy and war in the West. I was an avid chess player for years and I can understand why people use this analogy, however inappropriate it may be. Perhaps other martial arts may be like chess but Systema couldn't be further from it. Let's look at some of the characteristics of chess versus Systema:

- First, chess is very cerebral. It involves analysis, playing through possible scenarios over and over and weighing the possibilities of different courses of action, all with a given set of circumstances on the board. In Systema, we know that you cannot think and fight, you must act holistically. Thinking only stops you from responding.
- There is no physical contact in chess, only the contact of the pieces.

- There is no physical harm done when a piece is captured (although there may be some psychological pain, depending on the player).
- The pieces cannot react to contact — when contact is made the piece is removed.
- Each person takes turns in chess; it's basically a volley back and forth. Trading blows is not something Systema is about, nor do you have to wait your turn to act.
- Each person can take as long as he wants to move in chess (or at least until the timer runs out). In Systema, you must respond to be effective, usually sooner rather than later.
- Each person cannot move until the other person is finished in chess. In Systema, it is advantageous to disrupt the attacker in the midst of his attack, before he can adjust or complete his move and launch another attack.
- In chess you are limited to one move per turn, whereas in Systema you can create multiple moves to overwhelm the opponent.
- The chessboard, the terrain, is always the same, with clear boundaries.
- Finally, chess is fair — you both start with the same number of pieces and you can only move your pieces.
- To be remotely like Systema, chess would have to be radically different than it is played.

Imagine the game of chess played like this:

- You can be called to play anytime, anywhere, no matter what you were doing prior to the beginning of the game.
- You may have some or all of you pieces and likewise your opponent's pieces. The chessboard is a different design each game. It is a design that you only see when the game begins.
- There is no discernible distinction about who moves first.
- Each person can move his pieces simultaneously, as fast as they can without waiting for the other person to move his pieces.
- If the opponent moves to capture your piece you could move it to another square in the act of it being captured to save it.
- You could also move two pieces at a time, or even use your opponent's own pieces against him.

Of course, a chess game like this would be fascinating, if not impossible to play, but you would approach something a bit more analogous to Systema. Remember, you can't think and fight (to be fair you *can* think under certain circumstances); chess is about who can calculate better while Systema is about who can transcend thought.

Swim-stema

I don't know that I'll ever get tired of the new words I can create with the word Systema. Swim-stema just works.

My wife Karla has been a swimmer since early childhood and now has me hooked. At first, though, I felt like a fish out of water — in reverse. I've been "afraid to go in the water" since seeing the movie Jaws as a kid. This is not exactly true. Just open water.

I was fortunate enough to grow up with one of those aboveground pools common in big cities. Every summer we eagerly looked forward to pulling out the garden hose and watching the 4' pool fill with ice-cold water so we could splash around. Splash around was about all we did. The pool wasn't long enough for laps and we just pushed off the walls and glided to the other side, with a flailing stroke or two.

In the 5th Grade, I transferred to a grammar school that had an Olympic pool and a diving board. So I went through the standard "tread water for 2 minutes, don't drown, get across the pool without sinking" swim lessons. I even recall swim races that I participated in. Still, I never really learned *how* to swim; what the core principles were and the key success factors that would make me part man-part fish.

As time went on, I had fewer opportunities to swim. Being landlocked didn't help. Of all the elements, I've always felt an affinity for — and a healthy fear of — water, so when Karla came along and dragged me into the pool, I knew I'd get back into swimming. But the problem was still I didn't have the principles; I didn't know what I was doing.

Fortunately, Lisa Rapuano, a family friend, recommended the swimming book, Total Immersion, and the DVD Freestyle Made Easy, introducing a new style of swimming to us. Finally, I had something concrete to focus on to help my swimming instead of just flopping around envying those with the beautiful strokes wondering what I wasn't getting.

Here's where this ties into Systema:

It turns out there is a "hard style" and a "soft style" of swimming just as there are in martial arts. (Incidentally, the author repeatedly refers to martial arts masters when talking about swimming. I thought that was telling.) The Hard Style consists of just swimming, trying to bully yourself through the water on muscle-power and the perfect arm movement. After enough laps/miles you are supposed to figure it out. This type of swimming is more of the "dominate the water variety." Well, that just didn't make sense to me or seem like something I'd want to spend my time with. You might know some people who train Systema this way...

The soft style with the "new" stroke is all Systema. As I read the book, I kept noting words like flow, ease, grace and poise. The author talked about conserving energy, proper body form for the least resistance while moving through the water, moving from your body not your limbs, proper breathing and relaxation, and swimming like fish — that easily move through the water.

Stroke length and how far you travel on one stroke, is your measure of efficiency moving through the water. The fewer strokes the better; as you swim you get more results from less effort. It is very Systema-like.

Within a couple of weeks of working the drills and strokes of this soft style of swimming, referred to as "fish-like" swimming, I went from about 28 strokes per 25 meters to about 18, and a low of 16 strokes. I'm amazed at how much easier it is to swim, how much more graceful it feels and how much fun it is to just glide through the water.

As with all correct movement, my swimming is improving my Systema and my Systema knowledge is helping my swimming. If you're game, get in the water. If anything, it will improve your breathing efficiency. Soon you'll be ready for 3-dimensional Systema combat and fighting in the water.

Swim-stema – Part 2
Six Lessons from the Pool

Last time, I talked about how similar swimming was to good Systema training. Now I have a new perspective to add. I got the book, I watched the DVD and I played around with the ideas but I was missing one crucial element in my training. So I recently took my own advice, advice that I give to ALL Systema students and knowledge-seekers in general.

#1: I found an expert, not just some guy swimming or hanging around the pool. (Well, Dr. Karla found the expert for me).
What is the lesson here? Be careful from whom you take advice. Find someone qualified, not just the guy you are working with.

#2: Not only did I find an expert, I set up a series of private swimming lessons with him. I set up a series so the lessons would build upon each other. More importantly, I set up a series because I'm aware that you don't internalize all the teaching in one lesson. You have to hear, see and feel it several times for the lessons to sink in.

#3: I went into the first lesson telling him where I was, what I knew (or thought I knew), what my goals were and how I learned best.

We ran a thorough mental and physical inventory before even getting in the water. I told him I didn't come to swim, but to learn HOW to swim better and was open to whatever program he decided would get me to that goal.

What I didn't do was tell him all I knew about swimming, how I knew this method or that, or training with so-and-so. I made it clear that I was there to learn whatever he was going to teach. It's all too common in Systema for new students to come in and want to tell/show you all they know or learned somewhere else with little regard for what you are teaching them.

#4: I hung my ego on a chair at the edge of the pool and put myself under the scrutiny of his professional eye.

Here's a tip for you about "it feels right." I hear people in Systema often going on about how it feels. The thing is, when you are moving inefficiently your body adapts and the movements can feel right, even though they are wrong. This is where the professional eye comes in. He could see what I wasn't doing right no matter how right it felt to me.

Here's another tip. Whenever you train your body to move in a new way, it will feel uncomfortable because it's *new*. Sitting up straight when you've slouched your entire life feels "wrong," but intellectually we know it is right.

#5: I listened to his advice, tried it out, got more feedback and continued to make the corrections that he suggested. I can tell you that in one lesson my stroke improved as did my breathing. This is the value of an expert teacher with years of experience.

#6: I have follow-up lessons planned so my improvements stick. Learning isn't just a one-shot, one-day, one-weekend type of training after which I can fall back into bad habits or even create new bad habits.

If you are a Systema student without a home or a school to attend regularly, try taping your workouts so you can see yourself a bit more objectively. I guarantee you'll see things you would never have noticed otherwise.

So there you have it, 6 Lessons from the Pool that, if you follow them, will help your Systema as much as they've helped my swimming.

Swim-stema – Part 3

OK, I'm fixated on this swimming-Systema connection right now. But trust me, it's good.

My next swim lesson focused on my stroke and how my entire core — and thus my body — rotated along my spinal axis in the water while my arm extended forward through the water. This total-body stroke allowed me to move more efficiently through the water and to not fatigue so quickly. We focused on my body rotating my head to get air, as opposed to my head poking out of the water trying to find air, basically swimming with good Form, my skull connected to my body. It was an awesome lesson in body mechanics.

On to the experiment...

I spent Thursday pondering how to take the lessons from the pool and apply them to my upcoming Systema class that evening. It wasn't hard, actually. When I did Tai Chi, I learned that people refer to it as *"dry swimming."* Well, the same could and should be said of Systema, only more so.

We opened class with some ground exercises based on this idea of the arms moving the entire body along with them instead of disconnecting the arms from the body. That work progressed to taking this swimming movement to escape from grappling/ground hold downs.

Students had successful, amazing results.

We progressed to stand-up work, again with the extending arms rotating the body to evade, escape and position ourselves for hidden, effortless strikes.

Again, there were stupendous results. All in all, it was a 100% successful experiment.

A last word: Watch footage of Mikhail Ryabko at work. Notice how every time he moves, his whole body moves, how he turns his body while breaking the structure of, or striking his opponents. *"Dry Swimming"* indeed.

In the end, good movement is good movement — in or out of the pool.

So I took students through using these movements into take-downs, teaching them to not "root" and take down attackers from whole-body movement.

What are the results from this third experiment? Smiling students taking each other down with ease.

Success.

Explaining or Training

One of my fondest Systema memories is the first day of the first training trip I took to Russia. There was a small group of us with a scholarly translator who had never dealt with the military or martial arts. I didn't speak Russian and none of the Russians spoke English very well either. Yet we trained for 9 hours that day and my body moved better than it ever had since I was a child. Because we could not stand there and have every movement and idea explained into the ground, we spent our time smiling at each other while being knocked down and getting up. This day was a breakthrough, not only for my Systema, but also for the idea that training trumps explaining most of the time.

Fast forward several years. Yesterday in class I had several beginners who didn't know how to roll. This was a large class and I didn't want to kill time teaching beginners all the fine points of rolling. So, we began with a rolling drill where two people hold hands and roll together. Within moments, the new people were doing "textbook" rolls with their partners. One student, Debbie, said she had been practicing all week and this few minutes got her moving correctly — with no explanation other than to roll slowly as well as a demonstration.

Continuing with class, we did many movement drills — evasion and counterattacks to move into free-sparring. I performed a demonstration with Joe Malgioglio who kept breaking his own structure allowing me to easily put him down. As we continued — without explanation — it clicked for Joe and he kept his Form. It instantly became much more challenging for me to put him down. This small demo brought back realizations from that first training day in Russia.

Explanations and Joe's own processing and understanding of what he learned, only came later, at the end of class. Had all the explanations come first, he would have been looking for the principles instead of experiencing them. This insight is exactly what Paul, Debbie's husband, said occurred to him in class. He said when he stopped trying to do what I showed or said, he moved much more naturally and effectively.

What transpired in this one class, or any one Systema class, could fill volumes with explanations, break-downs, principles and fine details. Instead, we leave that class behind and move on to the next unique training session.

Explaining or Training – Part 2

So what purpose do explanations serve and to what extent should you rely on them?

As a teacher of a psycho-physical discipline my rule on explanations is just enough to improve performance. Anything more is simply too much talking and not enough work. Enter the "Karate Nerds."

The Karate Nerds are the guys who want to know, intellectually, all about the martial arts so they can have lengthy discussions and debates about the finer points of the art. They usually don't even seem like they want to practice, they just want talk about it. The Karate Nerds make the mistake of thinking if they can understand what makes the art then they have mastered it, as if memorizing the dictionary will make them Shakespeare.

This post facto analysis assumes that if you can reduce a work of art, martial or otherwise, to its constituent parts then you have mastered it. It is akin to analyzing all the notes in a Chopin piano concerto and then believing you can create one just as good by knowing them. In the end, being a karate nerd means you have an appreciation for someone else's creative expression, while fooling yourself into believing you can also do it by virtue of your explanation. You become a journalist, describing what the athlete just demonstrated more than a practitioner.

Explanations should exist to further physical skill; you should not have a physical art so you can create volumes of explanations. As soon as there becomes a secret code language for the martial art, physical training devolves into mental exercise.

Here is an example of the correct amount of explanation in Systema. "Keep your Form, don't bend over." This concise advice is easy enough to understand and apply immediately while continuing to train. In fact, most explanations can be made in the course of moving.

Explanation is an integral part of training but it should be applied judiciously. Always ask yourself, *"Are my physical skills improving, or those of my students, as a result of this explanation or am I wasting valuable training time"?* Reps matter, so don't squander precious training time with un-necessary explaining time.

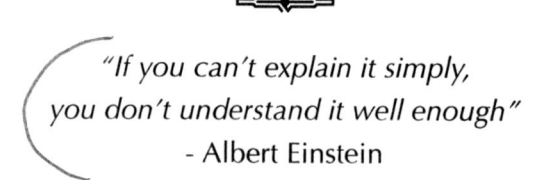

*"If you can't explain it simply,
you don't understand it well enough"*
- Albert Einstein

What Are You Trying to Achieve?

All too many times, I have been on the floor with a high-level Systema instructor (Mikhail, Vladimir and others), watched them demonstrate beautiful movement and then stood there scratching my head as I observed students not only using far too much tension, but deliberately doing so.

Were they seeing the same thing I was? Were they even listening to the explanation? Either way, they just weren't getting it, which brings me to my initial question, *"what are you trying to achieve?"*

There are a few reasons people are so tense and aggressive. Here are a few:

- Most people are overly tense and it just comes out in training. They don't realize how tense they are.
- They are trying to fight, in their minds, "realistically."
- They don't believe that you can get more results with less effort. They make up with strength what they lack in skill.
- They like to bully and overpower people with their strength.

Mikhail was once asked the first thing he would teach a new person. His answer was to teach him how to relax. Most people come into class tense, inflexible and not very mobile. The element of fear that most new students have adds to their tension. My long-time students always comment on how much easier it is to work against people with so much tension. This typical new-student tension is forgivable. With practice they work it out.

I had a student, Ralph, who was very tense when he attacked and was having a hard time relaxing when he defended. I finally asked him what was going on and he said he was trying to give a realistic attack. While that made sense in his mind, I told him that he couldn't simultaneously train to be tense and relaxed (it is possible, but he couldn't do it, and it was hindering his progress). In the end, he wasn't really giving realistic attacks, because no one throws a punch as tensely as he was. Again, this type of tension is forgivable, and we straightened him out.

A common situation I see in students is the *"Aha Moment."* This occurs when a student begins to move smoothly and escapes an attack. Then he sees an opening, a chance to knock down his attacker. At this *"Aha Moment,"* he suddenly tenses. The realization, and the thought of doing a technique, makes him over-eager and he uses far too much muscle. This is a common mistake and can be corrected with practice.

I had a student who was fairly skilled at Systema, enough to be better than beginners. He would toss them around but never let them work on him. He always wanted to prove how good he was and would fight other students all the way. He eventually hurt himself and had to stop training. I experienced this type of student myself in Toronto about 8 years ago.

I paired up with a rather large Russian student who spoke very little English. I was doing some disarms that under normal circumstances would have worked. However, he just kept using all of his strength to hold on to the knife. As we were alternating being the attacker I just refused to let him do anything to me. I just kept moving, kept Form and frustrated his every effort to put me down. He finally got the point and changed his tune when he realized I knew what I was doing. We did some nice work after that.

This type of tension is inexcusable, as it comes from ego and pride. I am blessed with very nice students. Really, they are nice people. It's hard to get them to hit people who need to be hit because they don't want to hurt anyone. They get frustrated when they work with someone with this type of tension. Sometimes even striking to relax the person just makes him more aggressive and tense. It's an unfortunate scenario as this type of person usually winds up getting hurt working with more advanced students due to his own tension.

I tell my students that they can learn to be tense, fight and struggle in most other martial arts schools. *"You can learn that anywhere."* Why would you even try to learn Systema and deliberately try to be tense and muscle everything. If you are trying to improve at Systema, you should be training to be more relaxed, more fluid and use tension judiciously.

I also tell my students (and myself) that if you find yourself getting tense unconsciously then back off because you are not learning anything. When you are training just ask yourself, *"Is this getting me closer to moving as skillfully as and with the quality of Mikhail or Vladimir?"* If so, then great, you are on the right track. If not, why are you doing it that way?

So, what are you trying to achieve in your training?

Remember you are not Vladimir or any other Systema practitioner for that matter. Your goal should always be "what can you do to improve your skills." Then train based on this knowledge.

Cirque du Systema

Systema is a martial art that can be practiced safely throughout your entire life span. I know many people who are well-past the age of "cage fighting", yet are exceptional at Systema. The breathing, relaxation, mobility and strength training keep our bodies going for as long as possible. Within the scope of Systema training is a subset of exercises that I call Cirque Du Systema, after Cirque Du Soleil, the acrobat troupe.

Fellow instructor Scott Meredith first put words to what I was thinking when I started seeing exercises that, at first were challenging, then became increasingly improbable for the average person to perform. While impressive, some exercises started to remind me of the circus and got me thinking, "What does this have to do with self-defense" and "do people have to be able to do this to learn Systema"?

Within every art there comes a point wherein the art becomes more "art," divorced from outside reality. Examples of memorizing counters-to-counters-to-counters to attacks that are low on the probability scale abound in martial arts. Of course, Systema does none of this, but there are some head-scratching exercises that leave people wondering, *"How will this help me disarm a knife at my throat?"*

I once saw a Tae Kwon Do demonstration in which the spry, young performers exhibited jumping, spinning kicks landing in the splits. *"Wow!"* the person next to me commented, *"That is amazing...but I could never do that."* He then moved on. That's called over-impressing.

Likewise, standing vertically on your shoulders and walking around, hanging from your chin on a pull-up bar, one-arm bridging, etc. definitely are things you see in the Cirque. Admittedly, these tricks are fun to try, but with limited training time it is more productive to focus on the core exercises that emphasize motions a normal body would go through during natural daily movement. There are other disciplines, like the aforementioned circus, yoga, parkour, gymnastics and breakdancing that will always surpass Systema on these acrobatic terms. Where Systema excels is combat and the majority of training should serve these ends.

However, the good thing about Cirque Du Systema, is that it keeps you humble and shows you that there is always some new challenge to overcome if you put your mind and body to it.

And now for a related question:

Q: Brad, do I have to have gymnastic-like ability to do Systema, like I see on YouTube?

A: No. For some perplexing reason, I'm drawn into this topic quite often. While it is true that some Systema practitioners can perform some amazing tricks, this is not a requirement for you to train in Systema, or to even improve.

Here's my take:

It is good to stretch your abilities about what you can do. A good teacher should show you the "possibilities" as some students are ready and able to challenge themselves at a definitely elite level. He should sow the seeds and each student should pick up what he can and work to move beyond what he's currently capable of. Don't necessarily expect to be able to do something that a teacher has been working on for months or years.

I remember Vladimir, years ago, telling me to walk on my shoulders for a seminar group. Disgusted at my failed attempt, he dropped to the floor and did it effortlessly. So I went home and practiced for quite some time to master this move, one that I'd never done before that day, much less in front of a crowd. I can do it and show it now, but when it was new to me? No.

There are some things he can do, that I'll never do, like hang from my chin. I don't need to. I don't spend time trying and the time it would take I could better spend improving other areas of my own training. I'm cool with that.

Just don't make the mistake of dismissing Systema because you can't do some acrobatics. Like Tae Kwon Do, adults see the jumping and flipping kicks and dismiss it as something for kids. There is much more to Systema and much that you can do, so get at it.

Improvised Knife Work

My wife stabbed me in the arm the other day with a kitchen knife. No, she wasn't mad at me. It was purely accidental. She had a knife in her left hand and a pot in her right hand. I, of course, was standing to her left changing a garbage bag. She turned suddenly and quickly to her right to put the hot pot on the counter and as she did so her left arm — the one holding the knife — jabbed reflexively right into my arm.

Naturally (thanks to Systema) I yielded to the tip of the blade upon contact; my arm and shoulder moved before I realized what was happening. I fortunately came out without a cut and just the sensation of being poked on my skin for the next few minutes.

Both of our minds were on things other than the knife and this brief incident occurred without forethought. We had a good chuckle about it and were both happy for my hours and hours spent in Systema learning to yield to a blade.

Training comes in handy in the strangest of places.

Don't Try To Escape What Grabs You

Last week we focused on some "basic" work, defending against wrist grabs. Conventional wisdom in many martial arts is to either "counter-grab," meaning to grab the person back, or to "go against the thumb" to escape the hold. While escaping and running is fantastic for children to get away from an abductor or for people taking a 1-day self-defense class and who want a simple, quick way to escape, for those of us who are training regularly in Systema there is a more effective way to deal with grabs.

Reason #1 not to escape. Pulling your arm out by going against the thumb puts you and the attacker on, at least, equal footing. What I mean is he has committed to an attack and so you pull your arm free. At this moment, you are both standing there free to attack. The grab can now become a deadlier attack such as punches or a weapon-attack. In this case, you have won the battle by directly dealing with the attack but not the attacker. Just yanking your hand out at the thumb usually does nothing to affect the attacker's structure or inflict pain. Dealing with the hold should ideally negate his follow-up attacks.

Reason #2 not to escape. When the attacker grabs you he commits his mind and body to the point of attack. This physical tension and mental focus are gifts for you to use against your attacker. The advantage here is you know where your attacker is, physically and psychologically. If you just pull your hand out you relinquish this advantage. For example, he may have broken his own structure in an effort to grab and hold you. If his structure is broken then one simple move can knock him down, without worrying about breaking the hold. The bonus here is while he is falling (or on the ground) you can break his elbow, using the tension of his grab for a point of support.

The Thumb vs. the Four Fingers. If you are concerned about breaking the hold, naturally you try to go against the thumb. However, if your goal is dominance of the attacker then working with the fingers is devastating. Just as the thumb gets you out of the grab, working against the flexion of the fingers keeps you in the grab. Here is why this is a great strategy. Working with the fingers means he can't let you go because the tension of his grab keeps him connected to you.

When you are grabbed, the attacker may be able to keep your wrist from moving but he cannot prevent you from moving the rest of your body. As you move, the tension of his grab forces him to extend his arm and body, breaking his structure. Now it's easy to knock him down.

A simple drill to show how this works is to have your partner grab your wrist. All you have to do is fall — lower yourself actually — to the ground against the flexion of his fingers, the direction his fingers would straighten out. If you do this with the proper relaxation, you will throw your attacker to the ground with minimal effort. Once you accomplish this you can then pull your partner off-balance without you, yourself, falling down.

Philosophically, working with the four fingers accepts the attack and works with what the attacker gives you to subdue him, whereas breaking the grab is much more of an oppositional mindset, resulting more from fear than an understanding of the attack and the attacker.

Everyday Gestures

Everyday Gestures That Can Save Your Life is the title of a never-completed book by American Kenpo Founder Ed Parker. As a Kenpo student, I was so intrigued by the concept that I eagerly awaited the printing of this book, which never happened.

Why am I thinking about a never-finished book?

Because the idea behind the book is so powerful that it was featured in a hit movie and now another new movie. I'll give you a clue — *"Wax On, Wax Off."*

Yes, The Karate Kid showed the world the principle that martial arts movements are no different from many ordinary, everyday gestures and actions. The current incarnation is *"Jacket On, Jacket Off"* in the Karate Kid remake, starring Jackie Chan and Jaden Smith. I've already heard people asking how that could possibly apply to self-defense. I can see many ways.

Mr. Parker got to share some good examples in his book series, <u>Infinite Insights into Kenpo,</u> as well as at seminars. One example was yawning and stretching. The action of moving your arms out could easily be a heel palm strike to the jaw. Another example was brushing the hair behind your ears. That natural movement easily becomes an upward elbow strike.

Mikhail Ryabko is a master of natural movement and of these "everyday gestures." One of my favorite examples was on a trip to see him in Moscow where he taught us how to escape headlocks and holds. At one point, he stopped the class and did a perfect pantomime of a child playing airplane, spinning in a circle with this huge smile on his face. He then had people attack him and put them down, one after the other, while laughing and making airplane noises.

In the movie, Mr. Han (Jackie Chan) says, *"everything is Kung Fu,"* and he's so right. I was taught, *"if it's right, it's Tai Chi,"* and *"Systema is just natural movement."* All good martial arts seek to reach this same point of uniting action with purpose.

For Black Belts Only?

I just had another of those typical conversations with a student and friend, Gavin O'Brien. The kind of conversation you get into all the time after you've been teaching Systema for any length of time.

Gavin moved from Colorado to Pennsylvania and naturally set up a Systema Training Group there. I've been in contact with him, helping guide the group and am happy to say he's on his way to developing a strong following.

Gavin recently had the opportunity to teach Systema to a Karate class. Here's what he had to report:

- The adults were "pattern-addicts"; they got stuck trying to do their techniques even where they didn't fit.
- The kids — I know you saw this coming — performed better than the adults because they had few preconceived notions or rules of behavior to hinder their freedom of movement.
- The Higher Ranking Black Belts commented that this

type of Systema Free-Form, Dynamic and Adaptive training is "For Black Belts Only."

There's so much wrapped up in this third response, I'll try to hit on the highlights.

My gut reaction when Gavin told me this was he should have said, *"For this class you are now all Black Belts, now let's get to the training."* Incidentally, when a new student boasts to me that he is a Black Belt, I tell him that most of my new students are Black Belts (usually met by confused expression). This isn't the first time I've heard this "for Black Belts only" argument.

The idea that a student should wait for 4-5 years before learning to improvise is ludicrous. Many martial artists exist in their own artificially constructed world with its own set of rules and dogma that no intelligent teacher would ever follow. As soon as they learn how to count, math teachers have students adding numbers to apply their knowledge. The goal is to be able to manipulate numbers, not just memorize them in order.

Even more telling is that young children acquire language in the same way students learn Systema — and they do it famously. (Check out www.rosettastone.com for an in-depth explanation of this learning process. I'm a huge fan of The Rosetta Stone language software and have used it to learn Spanish and Russian because this method works and gets results fast. Yeah, I've let my languages slip, but only for lack of practice not the method.

The funny thing about these "for Black Belts" arguments is I always hear them <u>after</u> the students have demonstrated their increased skills in one session.

"You can't do that," they said.

To which we respond, *"I just did."*

The proof of the pudding is in the eating.

So the "only for Black Belts" argument falls back to *"you don't deserve that knowledge because you're not a Black Belt. You shouldn't be able to do that because I can't."* I guess, through Systema, we are somehow teaching forbidden skills in their minds.

Who in their right mind would make students wait for 4+ years before they can try something that would help them in just one session? And, what are students learning in those 4+ years, if not how to spontaneously defend themselves?

Systema, Baby, Systema

I am back from a hiatus after having our new baby Siena Rose. That Systema is a martial art based on natural movement, would make it seem writing about the natural movements of a newborn a logical choice. I'll save that one for later. For now, I would like to address the movement patterns of a father carrying his newborn around and what is has shown me about Systema.

Many parents had advised me, just before Siena's birth, that having a child forces you to be efficient. They were referring to the efficiency of time and organization. I, on the other hand, immediately thought about the efficiency of movement. After a few weeks with Siena, as well as speaking to other parents about their experiences, I have noticed that carrying around an extra several, squirming and fragile pounds instantly forces you into simple and natural movements — kind of like the stick does.

The first obvious challenge carrying a baby presented was *the "I only have one free arm"* challenge. Normal people look at this as a burden, while I look at it as a training opportunity. In the first instance of holding Siena, I began to use every body part to accomplish basic tasks. I started using my shoulders and elbows much more to push, pull, hold, open and close everything around the house. I began opening lower cabinet doors and drawers with my feet, using my knees to balance things on. I even kept using the arm — and elbow and shoulder — I was holding Siena with to assist me as best it could with its limited range of motion. Tying shoes is a hoot! Of course, I had to accomplish all these tasks while keeping Siena safe, part of the second challenge.

Having a completely relaxed little body in your arms, makes for some interesting balancing acts. For one, the importance of Systema squatting has been indisputably validated. Whether holding Siena in my arms or in a sling, keeping proper Form when getting low is essential both for her safety and my back's safety. Any slight deviation of Form reminds me why you shouldn't lift anything with a rounded back.

As I moved around the house with Siena in my arms, I became aware that my spatial displacement just got larger. I am used to moving around and not bumping into things, but not with an extra head protruding from my chest. As I go through doorways, I have to account for the added space that Siena's body occupies so I don't smash her head into a doorjamb. So far, so good with no collisions.

Just moving around with babe in arms has been enlightening.

Babies apparently love the lumbering gait expectant moms adopt while in utero. So, naturally I get to ape this movement while soothing a crying Siena. This pendulum-like footwork and body movements are great Systema practice and they calm Siena down.

Everybody wins.

The Most Dangerous Close-Range Weapon in the World

I've been bashed, battered, bruised and almost had my teeth knocked out...*without ever seeing it coming.*

I'm talking about invisible strikes that came without warning, impossible to stop and darned near-impossible to wave off or roll away from.

The kind of strikes "you wish you could throw" at will, the kind of strikes you feel before you see.

I can guarantee you that I've not experienced this kind of Invisible Striking outside of anyone, I mean anyone, other than Vladimir and Mikhail — before now, and get this: *all with less than 2 years of practice!*

Now, you might be thinking that I'm here to invite you to some "special" training class so that you can tap into this amazing skill, but honestly, I'm still working on it myself.

I'm sure you're wondering who in the state could even have done this to me. Well, the answer is quite startling.

Siena, my 20-month old daughter. This kid has hit me harder and deeper from inches away with her skull — a skull that seems to be made out of titanium — than any Systema practitioner (again, other than Vladimir or Mikhail).

She hits without warning and even had me flinching and tensing last night while trying to put her to sleep. She's just that deadly with her Systema-Skull at close range.

No Tension, no Intention, No Defense. If I could harness this power like she does I'd be unstoppable. Well, it's something to strive for. I'm considering running a class to work on it. No joke.

When I say Systema is our birthright, Siena's head-butts prove it.

You Gotta Ask Yourself One Question

No, not *"do I feel lucky?"* I've been thinking about a very serious question, rather a series of questions, about Systema lately, questions I think you should also take some time to address for yourself. I'll give you my answers, which may help you as well.

Here are the questions:

- *Why do I continue to train in the Martial Arts and why do I train in Systema rather than BJJ or MMA?*
- *I am a smart, college-educated man, so what is it about Systema and other martial arts that I prefer them over MMA-type training?*
- *Am I daft? Do I not see the clear advantage of MMA training?*
- *Is it that I have too much invested in other martial arts training to give it up and do MMA?*
- *Is it age?*
- *Or could it be something else entirely? And are my reasons right for you?*

The simplest answer I've come up with so far is that Systema gives me the greatest chance to protect myself successfully in the greatest number of different situations.

Every martial art, somewhere along the line, gets niched; they all get specialized into a narrow context, like being in a cage or even being "all knife, all the time."

I happen to operate in multiple contexts. I don't regularly live in a cage, although home sometimes feels like a zoo. I don't always have a knife on me, although much of the time I do. I don't always need the deadliest, quickest kill techniques, even if I'd really like to use on them on the idiot in line in front of me.

The bottom line for me is I never know when or where an attack (or attackers) might come from, so I need to be best prepared to adapt to any eventuality. I need to be able to switch into self-defense mode in a split-second while keeping my wits about me to formulate the best response to any random, surprise attack.

Systema gives me the ability to use both instinctive responses, and at the same time rational, creative thought to deal with shock and surprise.

Systema allows me to remain calm under pressure, assured of my ability to (quoting Clint Eastwood again) *"adapt, improvise, overcome,"* faster, easier and more effectively than any other art or combinations of arts I've seen.

There you have it, the quick answer to *"Why Systema instead of other very effective martial arts?"*

You Gotta Ask Yourself One Question – Part 2

To recap, here is the main question:

- *"Why Systema instead of other very effective martial arts or MMA?"*

A mixed martial arts fight is about who is the biggest, best, toughest person around. It is direct "alpha-male" type of behavior. The idea is to prove who is at the top of the food chain. However, the strongest side does not always win wars. History is replete with stories of smaller armies defeating larger more powerful ones. Those who were smaller needed different tactics and strategies to defeat those who are larger.

If you are close to alpha male status — you are the biggest, strongest fighter — then it may make sense to focus all your energy on this type of event. Someone huge, like MMA Champion Brock Lesnar, well, of course, he would want to go head-to-head with anyone in an ego-contest. The problem with alpha-male thinking is just that, there is only one, like The Highlander. What about the rest of us?

I am 5'10" tall and 165 pounds. I fully understand that most people are bigger, heavier and stronger than I am. I can't even think about going head-to-head with such people. As a smaller person, I am fully aware that the problem I need to solve is how to defeat such bigger, stronger people.

The wrong question for me to ask is how to defeat the person in direct combat. The real question for me is what do I have to do to survive being attacked by someone like this?

Smaller people are often more dangerous because the stakes are higher if attacked, just as the smallest scorpion has the deadliest venom. Smaller people cannot afford to make mistakes or to underestimate their opponents. Therefore, they must have and resort to the most effective, sometimes deadly defensive movements. This is why I got into the martial arts in the first place. I was a small person in a large world and needed these skills.

I needed an edge, and trying to be the toughest guy in the room wasn't it. I needed the kind of martial art training that Systema offers.

BJJ offered (and still does in many cases) smaller people, like me, an advantage over larger, stronger opponents. But with the rise of MMA, it has lost some of its effectiveness because Americans are great at adapting and have created strategies for dealing with "the guard" and other BJJ moves. No doubt I'm a fan of BJJ/Sambo, but as I said last time, it is context-limited. It also still relies on too much struggling and force for my needs (that's why it is called grappling).

While this context is important to be comfortable with,

the nature of Systema training gives me other advantages. For one, the pain management work in Systema is unparalleled in the martial arts. The breath-work that teaches how to deal with the pain of being joint-locked makes it much easier to escape locks. The joint-strengthening and mobility work make it easier to avoid getting locked in the first place. The emphasis on breaking vs. locking makes it easier to neither struggle nor grapple. The nature of Systema striking is vastly different from the boxing paradigm, which makes it easier for me to debilitate a larger attacker without trying to box toe-to-toe. The major principles of mastering tension and relaxation to use an attacker's force against him without using much force myself has been the <u>major</u> reason I continue to perfect this part of the art.

Speed, strength, endurance all decline with age but the major principles of Systema improve with age and experience, and are particularly effective for smaller people like me.

There you have it, a second answer to *"Why Systema instead of other very effective martial arts?"*

Small People vs. Big People

An insightful thing happened in class last night. A petite woman (I'll call her June) took the class, the only woman in a class of about 14 burly guys.

That by itself is neither insightful nor interesting. Here's the interesting part: she is a Black Belt in a form of Thai boxing. The timing of her taking class coincided with an interview I just did about smaller people learning to defend themselves against larger people, what it takes and what kind of training smaller people really need. (See the previous chapter)

Everyone who comes to class for the first time naturally reverts to their previous training, and she was no exception. It's neither just good nor bad, that's just how it is.

As I watched her work with Paul who isn't much taller but much stockier — easily outweighing her by 100 lbs. — it was crystal clear to me that she couldn't rely on her previous training (or using it the way she was) to defend herself from him. The size and strength disparity was just too great.

Rooting and trying with lots of tension to knock him over wasn't working. Neither was going toe-to-toe with him. It was my job to open her mind up to different, more effective strategies of working against a bigger opponent, and I couldn't help but have a visceral reaction of, "that's really not going to work for you (referring to her previous training)."

Watching her try to thigh kick Paul encapsulated what seemed so, for lack of a better word, wrong about her training. It was like watching someone try to chop down a redwood tree — one that hits back. Sure she could kick hard, but he would just have taken it and knocked her out as she stood in front of him, trying to trade blows.

The idea that getting into a boxing, or kickboxing match is a good idea to defend against a larger, stronger opponent is not for me. Instead, I showed her how if she kicked him in a slightly different way, the kick would hurt (she could kick hard) *and* had the advantage of breaking his structure and knocking him off-balance so she could quickly gain the upper hand — without worrying about going toe-to-toe with him.

One bias of martial arts training is that students are constantly paired up with "someone about your size" to train with. This makes sense when a student is learning some new move because it makes the move easier to do. While this matching-partners-by-size may be great for learning a move, it is bad for training the move and testing it. Working only with partners of the same size also feeds into the mistaken belief that the same moves will work on a larger attacker.

Direct, force-on-force blocking a larger, stronger attacker is not the best idea for a woman, like June, to try — no matter how well these methods are marketed to the public.

To demonstrate, I had a large student grab some pads and swing at her full-speed, full-force, while she tried to block the strike. You guessed it; she got bowled over (and didn't like it too much). Next, I showed her how to pass the strike and avoid it without relying on force. Yep, this strategy worked like a charm, and by her look of relief, I could tell she'd rather not try to block the strikes.

Point made? Kind of. She never came back.

The beauty of Systema is that women are not taught to fight like men, nor are small people, like me, taught to fight like big people. No matter who you are, you are taught to fight like _you_.

Vanishing Martial Arts

I have a student who usually comes early to Systema class. As one of many people who came to Systema already teaching other martial arts for years, I still have a Kenpo class before the Systema class. This guy who comes early and watches class is a schoolteacher and a Systema junkie.

One day he says to me that it's amazing that he can see the Systema in my Kenpo when I demonstrate it, how I move and make it spontaneous. This is a good insight because I cannot "do Kenpo" anymore the way I used to before studying Systema — my body just moves differently, and on its own.

The second, more interesting, part of his comment was that he does not see the Kenpo when I do Systema; he says he just sees Systema. He says he has seen people who come to Systema from other arts and sees the Systema "overlaying" their other arts. But for me, after years and years of Systema, my other arts have disappeared. I take that as a nice compliment because that has been my goal since starting Systema — to have natural, spontaneous movement.

If you come from Systema from another martial art, then that's my wish for you also, to dissolve any pre-arranged training into the naturalness of Systema.

Lessons from the Second City

In case you haven't heard of The Second City, it is a comedy troupe that started in Chicago (2nd Largest U.S. City behind New York for years, and my hometown) way back in 1959. Second City was the *"training ground for a host of famous alumni including John Belushi, Dan Aykroyd, Mike Myers, Bill Murray, Gilda Radner, John Candy, Catherine O'Hara, Tina Fey, Steve Carell, Stephen Colbert, and over 500 more."*

Second City's claim to fame is improvisational comedy, as opposed to scripted and memorized comedy.

Sound familiar? Kind of like a certain Russian Martial Art you know about?

One of Second City's central tenets is that improvisational comedy can be taught...anyone can learn how to do it. We all see Tiny Fey or Steve Carrell and jump to the wrong conclusion — they were born funny. Nope, they were made funny through training. Sure, they might have had a sense of humor to begin with, but Second City honed it into razor-sharp wit.

The second tenet is that Second City has developed a

(gasp!) structured program to teach its students these improv skills. Second City has an entire course catalog on various aspects of improv comedy...made up on the spot....no memorized techniques...just comedy principles.

They even have (double gasp!) prerequisite courses before taking advanced improv courses....why bother teaching advanced skills, when the students don't have a foundation, or even been exposed to one?

Here are a few examples of Course Offerings: Movement, Movement for the Improviser & Stage Combat.

Movement

This is a fundamentals movement class in which the student learns to express themselves physically while using their instincts and intuitions. Basic skills like relaxation, stretching, and improvised movement are explored in this class. The tools obtained in this class will serve as the foundation for any performer's physical performance.

Movement for the Improviser

Stop performing from the neck up! Working through movement exercises will ignite your improv and sketch work with energy and vivid physical expression. Silent scenes, character exercises, and basic choreography will give you access to a wider range of characters to play and bring new life to both your independent work and work within an ensemble. Slow down the chatter in your scenes, penetrate the silence, and gain confidence with moving to song and music onstage.

Stage Combat

Have you ever wanted to learn how to slap someone, deliver a punch to the stomach, or how to fall without hurting yourself in the process? This is the class for you! This Stage Combat class focuses on the skills needed to protect the actor and their instrument when engaged in stage violence. A working knowledge of stage combat is essential to any performer's training and this class will give you those fundamental skills.

Prerequisite: Acting 2 or Improv Level B"

The act of improvisation relies on the brain's language centers, which makes sense because there is a "back and forth" just like a dialogue. In contrast, the act of rote memorization — whether it be comedy, jazz music or martial arts — uses different parts of the brain other than the language centers. This means there are two different skills being developed here. **It also explains why people who are good at memorizing aren't necessarily (and often aren't) good at improvising...unless they practice improvising.**

What Second City excels at is linking these two skills, learning simple techniques/principles and improvising off of them. Here is one exercise from The Second City that gets students in the improv mode:

"Yes, and..."

I noticed all the "yes, ands..." at a Second City performance years ago. I realized they were doing it, but at the time didn't know why.

Now I know.

First, "yes." Saying yes accepts whatever the first performer floats out there — there is no mental resistance to what the improviser has just been given.

No matter what the first performer says, the second person doesn't contradict it or judge it. It keeps performers from thinking, *"why did you just say something so stupid? What am I supposed to do with that?"*

In Systema, this translates into taking whatever the attacker gives you and moving with it, along with whatever first move your body makes as a result. It keeps you from getting mentally stuck and thinking what <u>should</u> you do.

There is no should. (Do or do not).

Saying yes takes out the initial tension and fear from the encounter. I often have my students also think to themselves, "huh? Now that's interesting..."

Next is the "and..."

"And" leads the performer into his rebuttal. It also gives him time to formulate a quick, witty response. He can latch on to any component of the sentence he was given and morph it into comedy.

"Yesterday my wife served me liver for breakfast."

"Yes and...How did your liver taste?" (In Scottish accent. me=my in this case)

The improviser had the time to focus on the word liver, and interpret "me" as "my," leading to the joke.

In Systema, the "and" comes from accepting the attack and just moving, anywhere. This acceptance and movement gives you time to find something, anything to work with and see what happens.

Not all Second City improv is stellar comedy. Some jokes bomb and others are mildly amusing, but getting performers to keep throwing things out there eventually gets the big laughs.

Not all self-defense encounters in Systema class are perfect. Class is full of "Let's try that again" and "partly successful defenses" that are good enough to protect you but not necessarily win the fight.

That's called learning.

Improv and spontaneous self-defense, as Systema teaches, both benefit from principles internalized and applied in specific situations, always building on success.

Be Undisturbed

My dog, Buttercup, is one of my best training partners for a variety of reasons. She is a Rottweiler, a good herding breed and a great watchdog (a little too good at times). She barks, from in the house, at any dog that walks by on the street. Her barks are very sudden, unexpected and loud noises that tend to elicit one of our reflexes and fears from childhood — the startle reflex, the one that makes you stiffen and jump.

Of course, this is annoying at times, but I choose to look on the training side of her sneak attacks. I have focused on breathing when she barks in my ear and, more often than not, I don't tense at all. Other times it is just one arm that tenses and the rest of my body stays relaxed. If I am deeply engrossed in something, or focusing too hard, then she gets me and I jump. I apply this directly into my training.

So what does this have to with Systema? Without exception, every high-level Systema practitioner has learned to control the startle reflex. This ability to breathe and remain calm even with sudden, quick or unexpected movements by an attacker is the hallmarks of excellent Systema.

OK, so you don't have to get a Rottweiler to practice this, but be aware of when your startle reflex activates, and when you are disturbed or frustrated. Practicing your breathing to minimize the startle reflex and learning to be "undisturbed" by surprise attacks and other shocking events in the world around you will improve your Systema drastically.

That Looks Fake!

My wife had a funny experience yesterday. She was picking up some Thai food for dinner and the guy behind the counter recognized her last name on the credit card (with a name like Scornavacco people remember it, for better or for worse). It turns out that he came into the school some time ago and I apparently showed him some Systema video clips of both Vladimir and Mikhail.

Although Karla thought he was going to have good things to say about the school, quite the opposite happened. He told her he was skeptical of Systema and joined a Shotokan school instead. He didn't believe that Mikhail could knock people down with just his body movements and shoulders. He never did try a class.

Recent posts on the Russian Martial Art discussion forum and my wife's own reactions to this young man's opinions of video clips have finally moved me to write a bit more about the subject of appearances, expectations and how self-defense is *"supposed to look."*

I was lucky to have never been subject to intellectualizing

Systema by watching clips and then judging it before experiencing it. My own exposure to Systema began without me knowing what I was learning. My good friend, Al McLuckie, was at my school in 1998 and was supposed to be teaching my students and me Escrima, instead he taught Systema knife work. I loved the work and was instantly hooked by how much sense it made. (See My Systema Origin Story)

It wasn't until after the workshop was finished, over dinner, that Al told me what he was teaching was not Filipino but Russian. I didn't care what it was because I was so excited to learn it. After decades of working at other martial arts, I knew I had found something that delivered.

Shortly thereafter, I met Vladimir and Mikhail and "felt" both of them. Mikhail toyed with me for about 20 minutes straight — I have it on video but am too embarrassed to let anyone see it — and yes I offered resistance. I thought that after decades of training I would have put up a better showing than that! As for the VHS videos, there were no Systema DVD's at that time, or YouTube for that matter, I watched the tapes trying to figure out what these Russians were doing to me, not whether or not it was fake.

As I began teaching Systema, people would invariably ask "what is it"? I have spent almost another decade trying to describe Systema to people and I still can't do it satisfactorily. I reasoned that if I couldn't explain it to people I could show them all the cool new DVD clips. This would keep me from having to explain it to people. Boy was I wrong!

Showing potential students clips of Systema turned out to be the worst thing I could have done. Either there were clips of subtle work with little contact or apparent effort, clips of brutal work or clips of people standing there and being punched. The people I showed clips to people were definitely not seeing what I was seeing.

Their views and opinions were based on either their own experiences or just their own pre-judgments of what martial arts "is." If they came in expecting to see one thing, such as stiff and rigid people in gi's struggling against each other and the clip showed something else, such as soft, fluid work, then they dismissed it. As for the brutal work and the striking clips — those frightened people off.

So I came to the same conclusion I have time and again, *"Systema can't be explained (or viewed), it must be experienced."*

As for video critics, who the heck are you that you are so special that Vladimir or any teacher has to prove something to you or it is invalid?! This is such arrogance. And this attitude presumes Systema people want to convince you, or are trying to convince you, of something. I, for one, don't really care what you think, if you are not willing to train in Systema or even get your feet wet and try it.

I came to Systema because people whose skill level and opinions I respected endorsed it. I have since seen countless people come to Systema from all kinds of backgrounds: police officers, bouncers, bodyguards, US Special Forces, former UFC fighters, high-ranked martial artists and on and on. These are all people with impressive backgrounds who experienced Systema first-hand and found value.

I have personally seen high-level martial artists, without ego, get on the floor and try Systema out, get hit by Mikhail... and learn something by stepping out from behind their rank or comfort zone. I have never seen anyone who actually worked with Vladimir, or Mikhail, got hit by them and say there is no value or that it does not work.

Vladimir once said that if you flatly deny something then you have no defense against it, but if you say *"maybe* there is something to it," then you are have a chance to respond.

Try Systema, then decide whether or not it is fake. You might be surprised by your own experience.

Can You Be Too Soft?

A man is born gentle and weak.
At his death he is hard and stiff.
Green plants are tender and filled with sap.
At their death they are withered and dry.
Therefore the stiff and unbending is the disciple of death.
The gentle and yielding is the disciple of life.
Thus an army without flexibility never wins a battle.
A tree that is unbending is easily broken.
The hard and strong will fall.
The soft and weak will overcome.
-The Tao Te Ching

One of the main training principles of Systema is relaxation, an idea that is often misunderstood. When people begin training they are already "hard and stiff." One of our goals is to soften students up by breaking up the tension, restoring proper range of motion and freeing up their bodies to move. A common mistake I see beginners make is becoming too soft, like a rag doll. They go overboard on the relaxed idea.

What they do not yet understand is soft and relaxed means no resistance, with only enough tension to get the job done and no more.

<u>Relaxed does not mean limp</u>. Being limp is being devoid of energy and lifeless; this isn't what we are trying to achieve in our training. Being limp is the opposite extreme of being hard and stiff. Overcompensating for being too rigid by being limp has the pendulum swinging too far in the other direction. This occurs regularly and is a part of the learning process, yet being aware of where you are on this continuum is integral to improving your proficiency.

I do a simple demonstration to illustrate being too rigid, too soft and then being "just right" like Goldilocks and the Three Bears. First, I am pushed and become rigid and am knocked off-balance. Second, I go limp and move so much I cannot counter. Third, I move with the correct amount of relaxation. Being just right allows me to move freely and effortlessly counter. This <u>middle ground</u> is what we are training to achieve all the time. Use this as a measure of how well you are doing.

So yes you can be too soft. Becoming soft is just one stepping-stone to martial skill. The next step after becoming soft is developing the internal power to be "solid" while not resisting incoming force directly. Remember, you are learning to be soft and how to move out of the way so you can subdue the attacker.

Jack-of-all-Trades, Master-of-all-Trades

Martial Arts are a niche-based industry. There are arts that specialize in striking, kicking, throwing, ground-fighting, knife fighting, stick-fighting, etc. Each art treats these sub-categories of self-defense as if they are disparate entities instead of simply the outward manifestations of the core principles from which they are derived.

Students of Bruce Lee's JKD recognize the limitations that specializing in any one art presents. Their obvious solution is to "cross-train" to cover the various specialties and areas of combat. These students face the herculean challenge of not only mastering the techniques of one martial art, but mastering the techniques of many different arts. They become jacks-of-all-trades. The danger is they often are not nearly as proficient as someone who studies just one of these arts.

The indisputable advantage of the JKD method is the students are well rounded compared to someone who studies just one art with one set of techniques. They are also much more open to learn from other teachers and arts.

A disadvantage to this method, and one I have seen

first-hand, is that students have to mentally jump from one art to another. I have seen teachers talk about going from their Tae Kwon Do kicks to their Boxing punches to their Wing Chun trapping to their Thai-Boxing clinch to their Judo throw to their Brazilian Jiu-Jitsu submission, all in seconds. Then, if you add weapons, they have to switch to Escrima-mode.

I saw a JKD teacher start teaching in sweats and a t-shirt, then put his Thai-Boxing shorts on to teach that, then put on his sarong to teach Silat, then put his gi on to do Jiu-jitsu. Didn't Bruce Lee say, "A punch was just a punch?"

The drawback here is this second-level thinking. Not only which technique should you use but which technique from which art are you supposed to use? You want to knock the attacker down: should it be the Kung-Fu sweep, the Silat takedown or the wrestling throw? Again, I have seen JKD students, in class, thinking out loud about which art they learned something from and if that is the correct technique to use in the middle of being attacked. Granted, this timeframe shrinks with training, but it is still there.

Having "no-way" as a way, as Lee said, is very different from having "every-way" as a way. Learning every art, in case you need it, is a Frankenstein-like amalgam of arts rather than a cohesive whole.

So how do you keep from being a master of just a small martial art niche, take this jack-of-all-trades idea and become, not a master of none, but a master-of-all-trades as well?

The answer is to dispense with the distinctions and second-level thinking. It's common to hear in martial arts circles that all martial arts are the same when you get to high levels. So why make distinctions at lower-levels? For example, young kids naturally kick and wrestle without ever calling it karate or judo. In Systema, we don't give names to rote moves. To do so would isolate the move and detach the movement from the whole of the art.

Martial arts should be seen as one trade and should be addressed as such.

The Journeys of ~~Sergei~~ Socrates with Dan Millman

Last month, I attended best-selling author Dan Millman's book-signing at the Boulder Book Store for his new book, <u>The Journeys of Socrates</u>. I also just finished reading the book and highly recommend it to all Systema students. Dan's narrative is based on Systema training methods and worldview, and is a great read. How did Dan learn about Systema and come to change his book to include Systema in it, and even make his mentor Russian?

The Journal of Socrates' Origin

In the summer of 2001, I was prepping for my second trip to Russia and got a phone call from Al McLuckie. Al told me that a former student of his, author of the Way of the Peaceful Warrior, Dan Millman was also going on the trip. Al told me to mention that I was a friend of his to Dan, because Dan was a really good guy and Al thought we would get along well.

I was excited because I came across Dan's book in Barnes & Noble while on my lunch break at the CBOE (Chicago

Board Options Exchange) in the early 1990's. I enjoyed the book and swiped its subtitle, "a book that changes lives," for my newly founded martial arts school in Colorado.

Dan was probably the first minor celebrity to take an interest in Systema and so received quite a bit of attention on the trip. Al was right. Dan and I clicked, sharing similar philosophies and energy. We had some good conversations before and after training when he told me that he would be staying in Russia after the training was over to do some sightseeing with a small group. I was also part of that small group and got to hang out with Dan a bit more. From Moscow, we took a train to St. Petersburg. From St.Petersburg, we took an overnight boat trip up Lake Ladoga to the Valaam island monastery, north of the Arctic Circle.

There are no cars on the island so we walked to each skete. On our walks, Dan spoke to me about his numerology book The Life You Were Born to Live, which I must admit I didn't quite buy into, and also about a new book he was working on.

The book was then-titled The Journal of Socrates and was meant to be a recording of his semi-historical, semi-fictional teacher of the same name. I tried to get him to re-title it The Trail of Socrates, a play on The Trial of Socrates, but he argued that no one outside of a philosophy major such as me would get the pun and rejected the idea.

Dan was enamored of the island, as well as Mikhail Ryabko and Systema. I could see the wheels turning in his head as he experienced Russia and the training. He said he was thinking of changing his book based on his experiences because he ran across something fresh and original on the trip. He decided to expand Socrates' training and lineage beyond the cliché eastern martial arts master character.

Dan's book was eventually released as The Journeys of Socrates. Socrates, was revealed to be born Sergei, a Russian Jew who trained with Systema masters.

Here is a brief bit that Dan read at his appearance:

When I was young, I believed that life
Might unfold in an orderly way, according to my hopes and expectations.
But now I understand that the Way winds like a river,
Always changing, ever onward, following God's gravity
Toward the Great Sea of Being.
My journeys revealed that
The Way itself creates the warrior;
That every path leads to peace,
Every choice to wisdom.
And that life has always been,
And will always be,
Arising in Mystery.

Do yourself a favor and pick it up.

Martial Arts Myopia

- *"We need Systema because other martial arts work, not because they don't"*

Myopia, or near-sightedness, can be lethal when it comes to martial arts training. Those of us who have chosen Systema training are especially susceptible to "martial art myopia" due to the rare skill level of our teachers and top students. Most students choose Systema based on this skill as demonstrated by top practitioners and conclude that the art is superior to other forms they may have studied.

This view, that theirs is the "Best Art," is shared by virtually every martial artist in the world. This belief is very natural because if you didn't think your art was superior you probably would not be practicing it. Who would admit to himself, *"this art I'm studying isn't very good, but the school is close to home"*? There are, however, some critical distinctions that you must make in any art.

The first distinction you must make in your training, Systema or otherwise, is that <u>you are not your teacher</u>. In

Systema, this means that you aren't a Russian Super Soldier (unless of course you are). In one sense it does not matter how good your teacher is; it matters how good you are. Your teacher, most probably, will not be there to fight for you if you are attacked. The faster you realize this, the better off you will be. First, it forces you to focus on your own skill level. You will have no illusions about what you can or cannot do. Your teacher may be able to fight off 6 attackers at once, but can you? Asking and answering questions like these will give you a true perspective of yourself and may change your behavior by changing your attitude toward a given combat situation. Second, you will be more apt to focus on your training and improving yourself as much and as fast as you can.

The second distinction that you must make is that your art is not the only path to martial skill. The common phrase here is, "it's not the art it is the artist." The real answer, however, is that it is both. Comedian Eddie Izzard does a schtick about guns. He talks about hearing that *"guns don't kill people, people do."* His answer is that the gun sure helps because, *"running around yelling Bang!, just doesn't seem to be enough."* Very funny stuff, but it illustrates the importance of both the weapon and the wielder. Of course, some arts are better than others at self-defense, i.e. are better weapons, but all arts are potentially deadly if you aren't careful. Even the smallest gun can still kill you, just as the person who has not done Systema can still hurt you.

Systema is a very potent martial art weapon, but never forget that there are others. There are people training in various martial systems around the world who are incredibly skilled practitioners. Even if the potential of Systema is greater than

MARTIAL ARTS MYOPIA | 143

other arts, they still contain enough weapons to hurt you. You can still be knocked out with a jab, choked, locked, thrown and kicked to the floor from the techniques people from other arts study.

Appreciation and respect for the skill level of non-Systema practitioners is the key to not underestimating someone's skill and correctly assessing your situation if confronted. I have seen several people who could not touch Vladimir but who have enough skill in their own art to be able to best most other Systema students or instructors. They have reached such a high level of skill, in their art, that it may surpass your own skill level in Systema. I have seen masters of several different styles who have never heard of Systema who demonstrate similar levels of mastery as high-level Systema teachers. Martial skill is available to everyone by birth and some people have just taken a different path to achieve it. They are to be respected for their achievements.

To cure Martial Art Myopia, it's a great idea to find a high-level teacher in other arts, or at least see them in action. Roll with Judo or MMA guys, box a little, work with some Filipino martial artists to see fast knife and stick work, even point-spar a bit to gain some appreciation of people with advanced skills outside of Systema. You don't have to train like they do, but the experience will give you a healthy respect for they can do. It will make you train harder and give you a chance to work your Systema against skilled adversaries. This is a great reality check.

Martial Art Myopia means not seeing clearly. When you label another person as their martial art instead of as a person you are not seeing clearly; you are seeing only the art, not the artist. Prejudging like this can be a fatal error. I've seen Systema people dismiss other martial artists after hearing the art they train in — bad habit. Respect everyone's training, respect them even if they have no training, accurately assess the danger your attacker/partner poses, and most important of all, learn from everyone you work with.

iRenew? Really? Come on

I've been meaning to write about this for awhile now and I can't put it off any longer.

Somehow I got on the channel with the incessant infomercials we all know and love, but this one caught my eye for its audacity and blatant misleading demonstrations. Now, I bought some Ron Popeil knives years ago and I have to admit I still use the steak knives and cleaver. That was actually worth the money, believe it or not.

But the iRenew? Come on...

Have you seen this thing? It's a bracelet that is supposed to give you some sort of super-strength, blah, blah, like Wonder Woman or something. Whatever ju-ju it's supposed to have with its super-duper waves, it's also supposed to keep you standing up when someone pulls down on your arm.

These demos floored me.

In one demo, the people are wearing the iRenew and the demonstrator tells them how powerful it is. Then, he pulls down on their arm, straight down into their structure and support. Magically, the iRenew keeps them from falling. (Eyes rolling)

Then, the guy pulls the unsuspecting people's arm — the one without the iRenew — down and back so you can see that they will fall backward. For a trained Systemist, it's glaringly obvious he is pulling in a different direction to pull people off-balance, iRenew or no iRenew bracelet.

It's the same thing we do in Systema to knock people over. I even felt compelled to show this hucksterism to Karla, and as soon as I pointed it out she could see it too.

What a scam! Parlor tricks. Bah! If that guy would have tried that on me I'd have adjusted my tension and put *him* on the floor.

iRenew...Nonsense.

Want some real "iRenew"? Get to a Systema Breathing Workshop.

Systema vs. (Insert Art)

I read an internet forum post recently that made me scratch my head. The poster made a comment that Systema looked like it did because it was Systema vs. Systema and not Systema vs. another martial art. He seemed to think that there is some person named Systema who was working against another person also named Systema.

Let me explain.

Martial Arts do not fight each other, people fight each other. In a limited scenario, the various methods people use to fight can be pitted against another a la UFC/Pride. However, in teaching I have come across some interesting facts about what the human body does to protect itself regardless of previous training.

My first observation came from watching Mikhail and other highly-skilled Systema people work with people from different martial arts backgrounds. First, I noticed that what Mikhail did was always the same regardless of the training of his opponent. What the opponent did, however, was different with each attacker, each attacking according to his own training background. The exchanges appeared different because some attackers rolled out while others awkwardly made it to the ground or fought to stay on their feet until they hit the ground.

Here is the fascinating part. Over time every attacker moved the same. The tempering process, which included plenty of strikes, made each person move the same regardless of their martial art background. I have seen this, and have been a part of it, again and again. I have repeatedly seen the martial arts techniques and moves distilled over time until they disappeared.

My next observation concerned the stick and the sword. Training drills where one person wields a stick or sword while others move around him trying to attack him also distilled movement into its purest form. Here I noticed the same thing as when people work with Mikhail. People would try to move in their stylistic methods, adopting stances, trying to use their hands and other tactics they have learned to deal with the stick.

But the stick is a good teacher and one of my favorites. It doesn't lie and has no emotions, no anger or sympathy, just the stick moving along its path. If you are in the way, you feel the pain, plain and simple. Hands that stick out to stop the stick get bashed, hard parts like elbows or knees that are in the path get dinged, and if you have too much ego and want to stand and fight then you get knocked out.

After seeing countless martial artists and beginners work this drill they always move the same way yet again. They keep their arms in so they have one distance to defend. They keep moving and breathing and if they are caught in a bad position they roll out to escape and survive, especially with the sword. Any martial arts system they may have been using disappears,

[handwritten: Movement, Breathing, Relaxation, Form]

giving way to simple, effective movements that protect the body itself automatically.

So what does this have to do with Systema vs. Systema or other misnomers? First, you are not applying Systema to anyone; when you teach your body how to move properly, it will. It is more of an "unlocking what is there" process rather than learning to apply artificial, external moves. If the attacker is attempting to apply a martial art and is tense or not moving then, as the Tao Te Ching says, *"the weak overcomes the strong and the soft overcomes the hard."* If anything, it is not Systema vs. anything, but rather this timeless principle of nature being applied.

In any Systema video clip, you see someone:

- Moving out of the way. (Movement) Everyone understands that if you don't get out of the way you get hit.
- Breathing properly to keep under control. (Breathing)
- Relaxing so as not to struggle or go force against force. (Relaxation) Everyone also understands that in force vs. force, the stronger wins.
- Maintaining good Form to maximize body structure and making it harder for the attacker to apply a technique. (Form)

Regardless of the art studied the person you see "losing" simply did not adhere to these principles. The particular martial "system" does not matter, the person applying correct principles matters. In the end, a person successfully applying these principles always takes advantage of or creates the advantage of the other person breaking them.

The Systema Anti-Principles

The Big Four principles of Systema have already become so commonplace as to be almost dogmatic. My friend, and fellow RMA instructor Scott Meredith, and I both like to challenge these stringent laws to expand people's minds and not pigeon-hole this art. Looking at the opposite of every principle or belief is an excellent exercise in critical thinking and can yield answers that you may not have seen before. Let's take a look at The Systema Anti-Principles: Don't Breathe, Break Your Form, Tense Up and Don't Move.

Anti-principle #1: Don't Breathe. Breathing is fairly straightforward. We need to breathe to live but there are exceptions. If you continue to breathe while underwater you will be in trouble immediately. This is one of the reasons we do exercises while holding our breath, either in or out. Poison gas, fumes or smoke from a fire are yet other times when breathing would be your downfall.

Anti-principle #2: Don't Relax, or Tense Up. Most people begin Systema training by learning how to relax. This is because most people are far too tense at the beginning. Learning to relax takes out "excess" tension. All too often I see Systema practitioners who are limp-they have taken out too much tension. A simple example of correct use of tension occurs when someone is trying to put a wrist-lock on you. If you are limp then your wrist bends and you are forced to try to escape the lock. However, if you put enough tension into your wrist so it stays straight then you have already thwarted the lock because the attacker cannot twist your wrist. The <u>selective use of tension</u> is the key to high levels of Systema work.

Anti-principle #3: Break Your Form. There is little doubt about the power of keeping your spine straight, which is why this is a fundamental principle. There are several times when bending the spine is also beneficial, such as when you roll. Rolling has a plethora of defensive and offensive applications. The spine, being made of a few dozen vertebrae, is well-suited to generating <u>wave motion</u>. This motion is predicated upon "breaking form" to work. Breaking Form is detrimental when the movement is linear, simply bending from one point. Wave motion, on the other hand, does not create a point of support for an opponent to work against.

Anti-principle #4: Don't Move. Vladimir gave us an example of when not moving is a good idea. He said that if you discovered you were in a minefield, moving right away would not be a good idea. Better to freeze and be ultra-cautious before doing anything. Any time you are not sure of your footing, or balance, is a time when not moving, then moving in <u>slow-motion</u> is the best choice.

The 4 Basic principles of Systema are guidelines because they work magnificently. However, the situation dictates your course of action. These principles must be understood in their totality and you must realize when the exceptions are preferable to the rules for your survival.

Sweet Home Chicago

Whew! I just returned from teaching a whirlwind weekend martial arts seminar in Chicago with long-time friends, mentors and fellow instructors Martin Wheeler and Al McLuckie. We taught a large group of cops, Joliet prison guards, MMA Fighters as well as civilian self-defense students.

The venue was too cool. The workshops were held at a place called Showtime, a nightclub that also holds regular Fight Nights. The lighting was dim, and was actually much better than fighting with all the lights on. It made it that much harder to notice weapon work. (I need dimmer switches at our school).

Here are just a few highlights:

I started the weekend off with an eye toward teaching Systema Principles that the students would then apply to everything they would do for the rest of the weekend. I taught "Structure and De-Structure" (yeah, I know it's not a word) and working in teams to take people down. This is all from movement.

Al fed off that to working some crazy knife-use. The nightclub people almost kicked us out because Al started using the benches and walls for some confined space work. That was funny! Al also worked how to effectively use distractions to set up knife attacks and counter-attacks.

Al warned students to "attack realistically with knives" so I took that idea and went on to teach how to deal with a knife attack when the attacker uses both hands, not just a solitary knife thrust. I primarily showed how to avoid the knife and work against the other arm to control the attacker. Al then finished the day with some striking work.

Martin took over on Sunday, again teaching knife defense in ways that few others can. He stressed moving and using your limbs as you move, instead of before you move as most people are inclined to, keeping your tension down while using the attacker's tension, and dealing with your tension as it rises in your body, among other things.

He ended the day with some superlative ground fighting demonstrations against both one and multiple attackers — bridging "traditional grappling" with Systema. Just brilliant work!

One student, in the end circle, commented that of the 4 Main Principles (breathe, relax, form and movement) the whole weekend was about movement. Good observation.

Paul Trout said it would be cool to see Martin, Al and me all teach the same topic to see our unique perspectives, how it all looks different but is really the same. Well Paul, we did it, it was enlightening for me too...and...you missed it.

A Critique of Systema

As **Systema has** gained popularity and become more widespread in America, the art has also opened itself up to more and harsher critics. The rise of video and the internet has been a doubled-edged sword for Systema — on the one hand it has exposed more people to the art, while on the other hand the uninformed can make snap judgments about what they see on video.

The Resisting Attacker Criticism

Why would any martial artists have to overcome a "resisting opponent?" To me this seems like a very low level of training — it means working directly "force against force." Martial arts are to protect you against larger stronger opponents, so why is it required that you must overcome a resisting opponent, at the point of resistance?

You cannot resist with your whole body while attacking. If you tensed your whole body you wouldn't even be able to move, much less attack someone. A good martial art should teach you to find the point of least resistance, or "the path of least resistance," and use it to defeat the attacker. The paradigm of directly opposing the attacker, then trying to impose a technique, fails to adequately deal with the strength and size issue.

Controlling the attacker's mental focus – as in the case of disarming a weapon – is critical to overcoming his resistance. Here are two points to think about when it comes to disarming a resistant attacker.

One, no matter what you do, the person may hold on to the weapon with all his energy and, in some cases, *"want to die with his sword (or other weapon) in his hand."* If you try any disarm from any martial art it will be next to impossible against this amount of resistance.

Two, you can cause the attacker to momentarily take his mind off of his weapon and then disarm it. There is a martial art saying, *"never disarm an attacker in his right mind."* This means that when all of his mental faculties are focused on his weapon you will have a much more difficult time trying to disarm him.

The task is to shift the attacker's focus off of his weapon-hand. The first way to accomplish this is to strike him. (A word about striking — this idea of focus and resisting occurs in striking as well. If the person is "braced for impact" then the strike will be less effective. On the other hand, if the strike comes to a place where the person is not mentally prepared for then the strike is more psychologically and physically damaging.)

Well-placed strikes, to body parts other than the weapon hand, inflict pain and shift the person's focus from the weapon. A quick follow-up strike to the weapon arm then makes it much easier to disarm.

A CRITIQUE OF SYSTEMA | 157

Martial Arts often talk about *"attacking the attack"* which usually brings you to force against force again. Instead, practice *"attacking the <u>attacker</u> in the midst of his attack."*

For example, the knife comes at you and you avoid it as it comes while striking the attacker. He is hit before his attack is complete and his mind deals with the unexpected shock and pain of the counterstrike. At this moment, his mind is off of his own attack as well as his weapon. Your counterstrike flows effortlessly into a follow-up strike to his weapon arm sending the knife flying.

In this example, you avoid a struggle to disarm the knife, avoid going force against force and do not create a resisting attacker.

People "resist" when they realize or are aware of your intentions. They resist because they sense you're trying to fight. Then, they marshal their power to this point, where the fight is, to prevent you from acting. Your ability to sense this resistance, muscle tension and mental focusing allows you to flow "around the resistance" to weaker areas of the body.

Part of what many martial artists don't realize is you can make the attacker more resistant or less resistant by your own thoughts and actions. Commonly, martial artists are so tense themselves that they make their attacker tenser and resist without realizing it. Then they have to find a way to overcome this muscle tension and fighting spirit directly.

The second way to take the attacker's mind off of his weapon arm is to unbalance him, creating some sort of takedown. <u>One of the *best* times to disarm someone is when he is falling.</u> When a person is falling the only thing he's thinking about is trying to regain his balance, provided he wants to stand and fight. He's not thinking about stabbing or holding his weapon. This is secondary to re-orienting himself. At this moment, he is most vulnerable. Striking the weapon arm of a falling attacker with any body part makes for a quick and easy disarm. In this situation you have created a non-resisting attacker.

The Over-Compliant Attacker Criticism

The corollary to *"The Resistant Attacker"* is a critique that hard stylists have over softer martial arts, that of *"The Over-Compliant Attacker."* *"He is just falling down, he is not resisting, that is not a real attack, etc."* Before I begin an explanation, I will agree that there are over-compliant attackers in soft arts. I believe that this comes more often as a misunderstanding on the person's part than the point of the art.

Over-compliant artists do sometimes *"know what their partners want them to do and do it too soon"* — I have had this happen to me. I know when this occurs and fix it with the person. There are other times when over-compliant artists are those who just don't like contact so they prefer to work to avoid it and bail out as a rule.

Both of these situations are the extreme, to the soft side. On the other side of the extreme are the martial artists who muscle everything and do everything in their power just to make your movements not work. These types are not trying to do anything themselves, just trying to prevent you from working. These are really two sides of the same training coin. They attack by running away, or defending, because of their fear. Neither learns much in their training.

"Neither help nor fight" is the principle that puts your

training where it should be. The first part about not helping your partner is a direct admonishment to not be over-compliant. Being over-compliant, or moving too much, is as bad as not moving at all. In joint-locking, for example, moving too much puts you into the next lock without the possibility of escape.

The latter part, about not fighting reminds you that if you begin to fight force against force, your own tension will be your undoing; your opponent will either overpower you or flow into another attack that you cannot follow and defend.

Imagine having to *"grab someone's attention"* when you want them to listen to you. The person, especially a child, may be completely unfocused and then by your voice or actions you bring them to focus on you. Once you have their attention you can talk to them and they will follow you.

This literal *"grabbing someone's attention"* is what happens in softer martial arts. Sudden, unexpected movements force the person to reflexively react and for that split-second focus only on the body part under immediate attack. Evoking this flinch reflex stops the person's actions and at this point they will continue to react to your further movements. This tension and grabbing attention occurs before physical contact is made — your reflex is designed to save you from actually being struck — and is what most people see, or do not see, from a video clip.

Another misunderstanding about *"over-compliance"* is the failure to understand just how <u>hard</u> good internal artists can hit and the effects these strike have. People who have not been hit by short strikes do not understand how they feel so when they see short strikes on video they don't understand why they make someone fall. Even though everyone who has felt proper strikes attests to their effectiveness people tend to doubt it until they feel it themselves. Personally, I have seen this in my own school countless times — *"all opinions change on contact."*

What's Wrong with Systema?

This is not a question practitioners think about asking because Systema has so many strengths. Some people may even think it is tantamount to a crime to even consider such a question. But everything has a weakness, some chink in the armor. It may be small, but it's there. It's better to consider it, understand it and prevent it from being your downfall.

I can see why people would fail to notice any weaknesses because Systema has so much going for it, so many strengths.

On one hand is the view to ignore any weakness and only focus on strengths. Often when it comes to improving, it's better to work on your strengths and let someone else help you with your weaknesses. But in the case of self-defense, there is no one else to help you and you must be able to protect your weaknesses.

Honesty and clarity and not fooling yourself for being shortsighted are all important for survival. Disillusionment is a positive thing and not a negative thing. It means seeing through illusion into truth. However, facing the truth about ourselves and/or our martial art can be both challenging and scary.

So, are you ready? Here's what is wrong with Systema:

- It takes a lot of effort to look effortless, and it takes a lot more effort to be truly effortless. People forget this, or never understand it in the first place.

Time and again Vladimir has said, *"Do honest work."* I've heard him say, countless times, to his partners, *"don't help me."* What he means is don't fall down when you don't have to, move when you don't have to, or purposely miss him when you attack. Giving a practitioner a false sense of confidence by being a "dumb dummy" doesn't help anyone.

The question you must always ask yourself is, *"would this work against an intelligent, resisting attacker?"* If your Systema only works on other Systema students (and skilled Systema students at that) it will only help you if you are attacked by another Systema student.

Not only must you think, *"Will this work against a non-Systema student,"* you must think, *"will this work against the non-martial artist as well as a trained martial artist,"* in each realm of combat. For example, would I be able to defend myself, with my Systema training, against a trained grappler? Or, would I be able to defend myself, with my Systema training, against a professional knife fighter?

Odds are that you will not fight another Systema student given how small the Systema community is. Take a look around at what is popular and what most people are training in: grappling and Thai kickboxing, along with Philippine and Indonesian weapons arts, and of course, Krav Maga. Can you defend yourself against a full speed, full force attack from one of these martial artists?

These are the type of fighters you will face; from the dawn of time has come the admonition to know your enemy as well as yourself. You must know and respect their strengths, as well as your own.

I say this over and over — you are not your teacher or anyone else in Systema. I call this the *"my dad can beat up your dad syndrome."* It makes no difference how good Mikhail is if some guy attacks you in the parking lot. You're the one who has to protect yourself because Mikhail is all the way in Moscow.

All you have to rely on is your own skill to defend yourself. It important to ask yourself how you would perform right now given your current skill set and not just ask yourself once, but all the time.

This is one of the things wrong with Systema. Way back when, everyone came to see Vladimir without any Systema experience, yet many had years of training in other martial arts. That has all changed. Now, seminars are filled with Systema students — the community has become somewhat insular. Systema students mostly learned to adapt to other Systema students. They're missing the opportunity to adapt to the different fighting styles — the way Systema originally developed.

Having a full-time school, I routinely run into people with little martial arts training and people with years of training and other martial arts. I relish the time practicing my Systema on all these different people. I spend more time with these types of students than I do with advanced Systema students. I'm always dealing with tense students, students who attack differently and the students who are aggressive and jittery. It is my belief that these are the types of people I would run into outside of the martial arts school should I ever have to use my Systema training.

I am under no illusions that self-defense will be easy, effortless, smooth and completely relaxed. Of course, all of these attributes are my goal and I continue to train with this in mind, but I will not be surprised if self-defense does not look like a demonstration. Another Vlad-ism, *"don't care how you look (and don't expect to look a certain way either)."*

Mikhail said at the first Summit of Masters, in Toronto, that he was sorry if he hurt anyone in his workshop and that if he were better he would not have hurt anyone. I feel the same way about myself, given my size and potential severity of an attack I most likely would have to hurt people to ensure my safety and the safety of my family.

Where Are All the Women?

No, this is not a chapter on dating. I've been asked this question several times and once as recently as last week. Here's my take.

7 Reasons "Normal" Women Avoid Systema Like the Plague

1) There are fewer women than men in ANY martial arts program. So if you look at it this way, every martial art and martial art school is competing for a much smaller pool of possible female participants. (This begs the question, why are there fewer women than men in martial arts?)

2) Systema is still fairly new to America. This means that there are **fewer Systema schools — and qualified instructors — for women to stumble into to train in, leading to fewer female students.**

3) Systema is still fairly new to the general populace. This

means that **people don't know what Systema is**, which makes them less likely to seek it out than another, better-advertised martial art that they understand a bit better.

4) "The Military" Image. **Because lots of military and law-enforcement officers use Systema it is portrayed as a Macho Martial Art, which turns women off.**

5) **Rolling.** Someone please help me out here. DISCLAIMER: I'm speaking from my experience teaching martial arts for decades and am not speaking for all teachers everywhere. I've seen that women, much more than men, have a huge issue with all the falling and rolling in Systema. I'm not offering any answers here, just observations.

6) **Striking.** Face it, we hit each other a lot and have lots of close contact. Many "tough-guys" don't like to be hit, much less anyone a bit more dainty, male or female. Normal men and women gravitate toward arts with less contact. (See the chapter: "We're Not Normal")

7) **MEN.** I'm not kidding. I've seen this over and over and over. Men treat women like they are going to break. By the way, this is the #1 complaint I hear from women — Condescension.

Or, they consciously or unconsciously, try to prove themselves superior to female students. I can only roll my eyes when I see this.

Watch any clip of a women doing Systema. It always comes across like *"look how good this person is doing*

Systema (for a girl)." Then, of course, there is the whole *"hitting on the one woman in class thing."* You'd think these guys hadn't had a date in a decade (well...).

So there it is. **The most unfortunate part of this dynamic is that Systema is possibly the only art that teaches women to fight like a woman and not like a man. Along with some BJJ/Sambo/ground-fighting, Systema is the Best Martial Art I've ever seen for women.**

If these 7 Reasons could be addressed, Systema classes would be swamped with women.

Can Women Learn to Defend Themselves in Just One Day?

1. What would you teach to women who had only one day to learn how to defend themselves successfully?
2. Is it even possible?

These are important questions that anyone who wants to teach women self-defense needs to consider.

Answer to #2 = Yes.
Answer to #1 = Systema, of course. (Did you think it would be anything else)?

I used to teach women's self-defense classes just like every other martial arts teacher — by technique. Women would learn a few cool moves that were more about getting them to think that they could learn how to defend themselves if they trained, than actually teaching them to defend themselves on the hurry up. Incidentally, there is a guy in town teaching exactly that — deep stances and hard blocks to women. Been there, done that. I can only shake my head. These women are getting "false confidence" that they could defend themselves.

Enter the LETHAL LADIES™

Lethal Ladies is the name of the women's self-defense program that I created that actually works in one day. Lethal Ladies has two main components:

1. Using body armor for Full-Speed, Full-Force scenarios.

Yes, a group right here in Colorado (Peyton Quinn's RMCAT) pioneered using armor. Basically, it's just glorified sparring gear, but it is necessary so women can "let it rip." I wouldn't recommend women taking any short-term self-defense class *without* body armor.

2. SYSTEMA.

Systema training principles are the key that makes Lethal Ladies unique.

The Breath Work to Contain Fear, well, you won't find that anywhere, especially not done to the extent we do it in Systema and how we apply it.

The Natural Movement Work is unparalleled in its ability to get women moving, escaping and overcoming their instinct to freeze. Honing their Innate Self-Defense Skills versus trying to teach them something foreign, can't be matched by any other training method, period.

I've been teaching Systema for 14 years and I am still astounded at how quickly these Lethal Ladies pick up the work. They are moving instinctively, spontaneously and pre-thought, all because of Systema principles.

I get a kick out of the marketing of Body Armor Courses because they are supposed to be so scary and overwhelming. Sure, they are for most people and they do work....

...However, by the end of a Lethal Ladies course, the women report being exhilarated and having fun. Just so you know, whenever I break out Body Armor for the Systema students they too report *"that was fun"* (fear and joy actually share neural circuitry).

One big distinction between the Lethal Ladies Program and other "adrenal stress" courses is that Systema teaches us to contain our fears rather than amplify them and try to harness that. This way we stay in conscious control while dealing with our stress response.

Systema's results speak for themselves, time and again.

(Caveat: we only dealt with standing grabs in one day. Obviously, other Lethal Ladies classes deal with ground work, weapon-defense, multiple attackers and the results are the same. I just don't want you to think training is ever finished after one day, it's just that the progress is amazing!)

Women, Systema & Body Armor

Periodically, at the school, we teach a Full-Force Women's Self-Defense Course. One of the elements of this course is that we have guys in protective body armor attack the women at full speed and strength. For those who have never been attacked, this can be a traumatic experience. This is where Systema comes in.

I taught this course before I trained in Systema myself and have since changed much of it. One very noticeable addition has been teaching proper breathing. Before Systema, we did not focus on breathing to control the fear response or to recover from the stress of the assault. It was more of "here it comes, deal with it."

During last Saturday's class, it was enlightening to see how teaching breathing helped the women keep their wits about them, still being able to think while they fought and normalized themselves after the assaults. Breathing helped shift the focus from reinforcing the stress responses and the damage it does to the body to minimizing the deleterious effects of repeated stress on the body.

Besides the breathing, we now teach many of the Systema movement and escape drills to the women, including mass attack work. It is amazing to see women who practice the natural movements for less than one hour, apply them immediately to move and escape while under a full-speed, full-power attack. I have seen other courses that include an armored attacker who is basically a human punching bag, i.e. he only yells and stands there, waiting to be hit. The women Saturday were fighting all-out against a fully interactive, larger attacker and they performed admirably.

As to the incessant question, *"Does Systema work at full speed"?* Even after only one day, with brand-new women learning it the answer is, as we all know, a resounding YES!

Are You Ready for the Indy 500?

I was talking to a friend and Systema Instructor the other day, and I asked him this question:

"Why can't I drive in the Indianapolis 500?"

"(Censored answers here)"

"No because I've never driven that fast in my life. But if they were all driving 55 mph, I could drive with any of them."

"I sense a Systema analogy coming on."

"If I continued to drive like I did when I learned as a teenager, I'd still be driving around parking lots at 5 mph with my Driver's Ed teacher...."

We have a mix of students in my classes, from those with zero experience to guys with extensive martial arts experience in various forms, and I like to ramp up the training. But, is it fair to make the newbies try to defend themselves full-speed from the types of attacks the more experienced guys are used to throwing at them? Is it fair to always make the experienced guys figuratively drive at 5 mph with the newbies?

The answer in both cases is no and that there are better training methods everyone should be using because each student should be preparing for the martial art equivalent of the Indy 500 — an all-out fight with one or more attackers with weapons, standing, on the ground and all-around.

There are simple ways to structure your training, like we do in my classes, to be able to increase speeds and insure you aren't ingraining bad habits while proving to yourself *"you have what it takes"* to work effectively at speed. Here's one way to do it:

The Speed Pyramid

Once students have spent some time and energy practicing a certain topic or scenario slowly, it's time to ramp up the speed. In this test drill, one student will attack the other 9 times in a row, from slow motion to full-speed back down to slow motion. I just count out the numbers and my students know how fast to attack.

The Speed Pyramid gives students instant feedback about how well they can perform effectively, and at what speed. It also brings to light whatever mistakes or bad habits that students have and allows us to fix them in future classes.

Don't give me the *"it's too dangerous to train fast"* line because everyone in my classes comes out fine, with nothing worse than a few nicks and scrapes. We've proven it's as safe as any other training method, if not safer.

5 mph looks different from 55 mph, and 55 mph looks a lot different from 155 mph and more. If you haven't experienced each of these speeds and learned to operate at the various speeds how can you ever hope to do so under the stress of attack? And don't give me the *"but Vladimir can"* line either, because he won't be driving (fighting) for you.

So, are <u>you</u> ready for the Indy 500?

The Speed Pyramid

- 1 = slow motion
- 2 = 25% of attacker's full-speed
- 3 = 50% of attacker's full-speed
- 4 = 75% of attacker's full-speed
- 5 = Full-Speed
- 4 = 75% of attacker's full-speed
- 3 = 50% of attacker's full-speed
- 2 = 25% of attacker's full-speed
- 1 = slow motion

You Can Go Your Own Way

Over the years, I've seen quite a few instructors and prominent students leave my Systema lineage, for another Russian Martial Art teacher, for another martial art altogether or to form their own organizations. Each of these actions is fairly common with students, and not just in the martial arts. Perhaps it is inevitable. Personality clashes and philosophical differences are just two of many reasons that people choose to dissociate with each other.

Recently I've received inquiries as to why a prominent Systema Instructor (and friend of mine) would choose to leave and do his own thing. I've been thinking about it quite a bit and have been curious as to people's reactions to his decision. I could write a whole book on his decision but I'll highlight a few salient points here.

We all come to teachers, martial arts or otherwise, for certain personal benefits. Both the teacher and the teachings should serve us, not vice versa. If they don't, then it's time to find something and/or someone that does.

"You are not the martial art you study." I've run into this

over and over again — people defining themselves through their martial art, as their art. You are not your martial art. You are a person who does a martial art, or whatever. If Systema doesn't work for you, find something else that does. No big deal. I've had many students who are better served with other martial arts, which is why I teach them something other than Systema.

A person who seeks to reach his potential and *"be his own person"* cannot be slave to titles or particular systems. As William Blake said, *"I must create my own System or be enslaved by another man's. My business is not to reason and compare; my business is to create."*

Everyone's path is different. It is neither my, nor your, place to judge others, only to offer help if asked and wish him the best of luck.

If you are secure on your path, be it Systema or something else, then you will wish him and others well and get on with your own training. You don't have to make him wrong for you to be right.

"If only the best birds sang, the world would be silent." Some would argue that he is not as good as his teachers so how could he leave. If staying is not making him better, it is the wrong thing to do. If leaving will make him better then it is the right thing to do. There is always someone better — artists, painters, musicians — yet all skilled practitioners have something to contribute, and they should.

High-level martial artists are notoriously individualistic and it is no surprise that *"there are too many chiefs, not enough Indians (indigenous people)."* I see this everywhere martial artists try to create organizations. The Extraordinary is always going his or her own way. Don't expect anything else.

Systema GrandMasters should teach what no one other than they can do. This is their uniqueness and they need to show it to the world. They should not be faulted for displaying their skill. However, students may need a variety of (and different) training methods and experiences to hope to get to, or even close to, their level. This may take a lifetime, as well as other influences to achieve.

I could go on, but I have other things to write...

Systema, over the years, has become somewhat "codified" as to what IS and what ISN'T Systema. What used to be fostered as, "your own interpretation" has become more of a party-line kind of thing. To paraphrase Bruce Lee, *"JKD (Systema) is just a name, don't make too much of it."*

The students at my school have seen my own way develop and often hear me say that if I ever made a martial art up I'd call it, *"I don't give a #$%& what you call it."* To put it another way, *"if there were only one diet there would be only one diet book. But there isn't."*

Systema Hubris

I promised you a Short Stick Story and I'm not one to go back on my word, so here it is:

Several years back (around 2001), I met a few gentlemen on a trip to Russia. They were relatively new to Systema at the time and characteristically excited about this amazing martial art. Nice guys, but I didn't see or hear much from them after the trip — other than a website that popped up showing Systema schools now in a bunch of places around their home town. Ok.

The world is full of really good martial artists with tons of experience who are really good martial artists with tons of experience that like to go to "open mat, share-your-art" kind of events. Apparently, one of these "Systema converts" goes up to a guy with a short stick in his hand and says, *"Let me show you why Systema is better than what you're doing. Just come at me with that stick however you'd like."*

Before I tell you what happened, it's important to keep in mind that:

1) You are not Mikhail Ryabko or Vladimir Vasiliev.
2) The world is filled with bad dudes who love to scrap.
3) If a guy is swinging a stick, he probably really likes that weapon and might, just might, know how to use it.
4) You are at a distinct disadvantage by not having a weapon yourself.
5) Especially if you've never been on the receiving end of a Full-Speed, Intelligent Stick Attack.

So, I'm sure you guessed it...

The guy with the stick accepted the challenge, came at him full-speed, with decades of full-contact stick fighting under his belt, and proceeded to beat this "deluded Systema guy" into the ground.

Hubris gets you every time.

The Danger of Having a Martial Artist for a Father

When people see my daughters — how cute they are (ok, I'm biased) - they immediately say things to me like, "I can't wait until they bring home a boy and the kid learns what you do for a living."

That is not the kind of danger of having a martial artist for a father that I'm talking about, but I will talk about that particular one later.

What I am talking about is incidents like this one:

Petra runs headlong at my leg, trying to knock me over. Without her realizing it, my leg has moved out of the way and she falls face down on the hardwood floor and bursts into tears.

I can't help it, really.

I've spent decades training to prevent people from slamming into my body, for my own safety. We call it not giving an attacker "support," or anything to hold on to and fight against. She expects impact, and when it doesn't come she cannot stop herself from falling over. This is a coveted, high-level martial arts skill.

The best way I can describe this skill is as **The Peanuts Principle**. Lucy holds a football that Charlie Brown sets up to kick. Precisely when Charlie Brown is about to kick the football Lucy pulls it away and poor Charlie Brown flips in the air and lands on his back with a pathetic, humorous thud. Lucy's timing is perfect.

That's the danger my girls face, right now, from having me as a dad. They run at, jump on and lean into me and I instinctively "pull the football away" and they wind up smashing into the couch.

I am getting better at letting them slam into me, sacrificing my body to keep them from screaming, but I must admit that I do get an abnormal feeling of "wow, that was so cool," whenever I reflexively avoid them, causing them to fall down without ever touching them. (Did I mention we're not normal?)

I can't help it, really.

That's what my martial arts training is all about. That feeling of demonstrating the perfect timing is intensely gratifying. Yet, at the same time I have to hurry and pick them up from the floor, comfort them and kiss their "owie." I'm emotionally torn.

And I feel horrible.

The same sort of thing happens with my wife when we go dancing. Whenever I twirl her around, automatically I want to spin her right to the floor. Not consciously mind you, my body wants to change the angle of the spin just enough so she loses her balance and take a tumble. It's a habit, and a good one under different circumstances. And no, that's not simply an excuse so I don't have to take her dancing.

Just last weekend we were dancing and I had to move her out of the way of another couple, so I did what came natural and guided her out of their way as fast as I could. She said I almost broke her wrist.

I should come with some kind of warning label.

How Can I Make Him See How Cool Systema Is?

I get so many questions that I can barely remember them all, but yesterday I got a doozy...and I think it pertains to most Systema teachers and practitioners. Ron Jesser comes to class and is blown away by Systema, after having researched it and talked to my buddy Sonny on Facebook. He has a teenage son and asked me this question:

- *"My 15 year old son wants to be a champion MMA fighter. How do I get him to understand that Systema is much more practical and how he should train?"*

I'm sure that if you're like most Systema people you'd go into a long tirade about how amazing Systema is, but that's not how I answered.

First, the kid is 15. I told Ron that it is the difference between ego and survival. His son is young and full of competition-hormones. He wants to be the best. Who wouldn't understand that possibly this kid may have the need to get out and compete and prove something. Most adults have competed in something, if not martial arts contests.

Second, there are plenty of skills and knowledge to be gained from MMA training, especially at the school the kid is going to — it's a good school. The idea that MMA doesn't work "outside the ring" is a grave mistake.

Third, I told Ron how I could take the grappling that his son is learning and "Systema-ize" it to make him even better, more relaxed, strike harder, escape easier, etc., when he is ready. When Ron goes and shows him what he learned in Systema class, I'm sure his son would see the benefits to his own training.

In the end, Sytema is <u>not</u> for everyone (I'll go so far as to say it's not for most people). Yes, it can benefit everyone, but people need to go through whatever it is they have to. When they are ready for Systema, well, there's no going back.

As in all things, it is best to leave them alone and perhaps gently guide them to give Systema a chance — at least to see how it can improve what they are already doing.

Forcing someone to train Systema is just like forcing a technique on a situation that doesn't warrant it. It just doesn't work.

Systema Magic

A further critique of Systema is that it is just magic. This is often said or written with a derogatory tone. I take umbrage with this criticism because I have great respect for magic, particularly close-up magic that requires countless hours of practice.

When people see a magic trick performed properly they are amazed. They instantly want to know, "how did he do that"? They know intuitively that there is a simple explanation about what they just saw but they just cannot figure it out. They don't know the secret of how it works, but they know it works. A magician spends hours, days, months and years practicing his craft so that it is smooth and deceptive. They even take an oath not to demonstrate a trick that they cannot perform with absolute success, so as not to give away the trick's secret.

Years ago, I had my watch stolen right off my wrist. I only got it back because the guy was a magician and an expert pickpocket. I knew it was possible because the guy had just done it. What I wanted to know was, how? How could a guy touch me, without me knowing it and take a clasped watch off my wrist? This wasn't just lifting a loosely held wallet out of a jacket pocket. How?

I've watched Mikhail Ryabko "pickpocket" knives right out of attackers' hands as they stand there and laugh...until he punches them in the jaw. I've seen this time and time again. Attacker has the knife, now Mikhail has the knife. I see the same baffled expression on the attacker's face every time.

How is Mikhail disarming a knife-wielding attacker any different from stealing a watch off of my wrist?

I've also been in a straitjacket, but not in a padded room. A presenter was escaping from a straitjacket trick as a metaphor for getting "unstuck" in life. After he escaped, I asked if I could try; I couldn't escape. Here again, I *knew* there was a way out even if I couldn't figure it out for myself. Then he shared the secret, which entails several different body movements. In Systema we use these same movements to create space where none seemingly exists and to escape from holds.

How is an escape from a straitjacket any different from an escape from a bear hug?

Magic uses our senses and thought processes against us, to astound us. Magic relies on illusions, sensory and cognitive, to baffle an audience. Magic takes advantage of the brain's predictive nature, sets up these predictions, then violating these predictions thereby creating the magic effect. Magicians also toy with your attention, controlling what you sense and what you think you sense. Magicians know that we see what we expect to see, not what is really there.

Consider this: one key to a magician's success is using natural, innocuous movements that allow them to hide cards without drawing attention to it, while at the same time drawing the spectators' attention to some other action. Magicians can literally make you fail to see what is right in front of your eyes, creating "inattention blindness."

Watch Mikhail raise his fist "right in front of an attacker's face," without them reacting at all. He does so naturally and without tension. The attacker's brain doesn't register the natural movement as threatening so it dismisses the movement. The short punch comes as a total surprise. Couple this movement with a smiling face that takes advantage of "joint attention," and you can see how no one ever sees the punch coming. Attackers feel Systema punches before they see them.

Or consider this: a common magic trick is to make a salt shaker pass through a table. The trick starts with the salt shaker being covered by a napkin, which assumes the shape of the salt shaker. The magician pounds the napkin, striking the saltshaker through the table, which he produces from under the table in his other hand. Magic.

The secret of this trick is that the magician surreptitiously drops the saltshaker over the edge of the table, into his lap while he misdirects and distracts the audience. The napkin maintains the shape of the saltshaker so, naturally, the audience assumes it's still there. This assumption, along with the sound of banging the table, makes the illusion work. The audience sees and hears what they expect to experience, not what is really there (or not there).

Your brain assumes that an object has the properties, such as weight and density that every object in its class has. If it looks like a bottle and an actor hits another actor over the head with it, you assume the bottle was hard — just like all other bottles — and not made of sugar, which this one is. The same is true of people, and Systema takes advantage of this cognitive shortcut.

When someone attacks us, his brain assumes that we are solid and heavy. His body predicts & expects a certain response and braces itself for impact. We routinely violate this expectation by moving lightly, with perfect timing so that no collision occurs. By the time the attacker can adjust, it is too late. The incredulous refrain the attacker gives is, *"he's not there, he's like a ghost, I couldn't feel a thing."*

I suggest reading, The Secret Life of Houdini. Not only is it an excellent read, you will learn how much time and energy Houdini put into creating his escapes as well as some of the specific skills he taught himself. Isn't reading about The World's Greatest Escape Artist a good idea when learning how to escape from holds?

Systema is Magic and Magic is Systema, and it's all natural.

Martial Jazz

I am a musician, a pianist who loves jazz. Systema is Jazz, Martial Jazz. The extemporaneous playing, the back-and-forth riffing on each other's melodies and the individual expression, it's all the same. I found a fascinating blog entry by Trent Harris on www.JazzConspiracy.com comparing jazz music to martial arts. Recognizing the link between Systema and jazz, it is nice to see people on the jazz side also seeing the connection. While Harris comes at his analogy from martial arts to jazz, I suggest looking at the analogy from jazz to martial arts as well. I also recommend watching the documentary on jazz by Ken Burns.

Bruce Lee: Jazz Giant

"Normally, we don't think of jazz and martial arts together, but to me, martial arts serve as a metaphor for jazz. After watching Enter the Dragon with Bruce Lee, I began to see that both martial artists and jazz artists deal with many of the same issues in practice and performance. For example, improvisation is a central pillar of both arts.

Also, in both arts one practices very methodically and with discipline, in order to perform very spontaneously and unpredictably!"

- Trent Harris

On the Nature of the Artistic Pursuit:

Bruce Lee: So in other words what I'm saying therefore is that he's paying me to show him in combative form, the art of expressing the human body.

Lesson: Jazz is about music, but it's about a lot more. Yes, we learn to play instruments and songs. But it's also about exploring, experimenting, journeying, discovering, and expressing yourself through the art of jazz.

Bruce Lee: But to express oneself honestly, not lying to oneself, and to express myself honestly now; that, my friend, is very hard to do and you have to train.

Trent Harris: Great jazz, just like great martial arts, isn't about showing off, and it isn't about ego. It's about being true to yourself and the people around you, and being real.

On Artistic Styles:

Bruce Lee: Because of style, people are separate. They are not united together because style became law. But the original founder of the style started out with hypotheses. (scoffs) But now it has become the gospel truth. And people that go into it man, became the product of it.

Trent Harris: Jazz and martial arts have both been fractured by sub-genres, but this after-the-fact segmentation misses the point. There shouldn't be an argument between Dixieland, Bebop, Cool, Post-bop, Free, Latin, or Fusion about which is best, any more than there should be a battle between Karate, Tae Kwon Do, Jujitsu, Greco-Roman Wrestling, Judo, and so on. If all you try to do is be a "style", then you're selling yourself out. Don't get caught up in styles. Each style has its own place in terms of being a way of expressing the human self. Each one is appropriate and "right", depending on the circumstances. It's about the music. Play whatever best lets you express what's in your soul, plain and simple. **If you can do that, it's right, and it doesn't matter what style people want to call it, because it's you.**

On Learning by Imitation versus Cultivation of Individuality:

Bruce Lee: When I look around, I always learn something, and that is, to be always yourself and to express yourself, to have faith in yourself. Do not look for a successful personality and duplicate it.

Trent Harris: The best jazz and martial artists are those who are able to master styles and technique, and then transcend it by using it as a tool to develop, come into, and express their unique musical personality and self. That's what separates the great jazz artists from lesser jazz artists.

On Spontaneity versus Control:

Bruce Lee: So therefore it is not only, it is not pure naturalness or unnaturalness. The ideal is unnatural naturalness, or natural unnaturalness. (smirks)

Trent Harris: A jazz artist, just like a martial artist, needs a lot of technique, structure, and control to be able to perform. But this by itself isn't enough. You also need a certain amount of creativity, disorder, and surprise to keep things interesting. **So it's a balancing of the two – you need technique and discipline, but also creativity, spontaneity, and willingness to break the rules and do the unexpected.**

On Some of the Traits of a Great Artist:
Bruce Lee: Empty your mind. Be formless. Shapeless. Like water.

Trent Harris: To a certain extent, martial artists and jazz musicians must be "shapeless." They must always be mentally present, in the moment, able to roll with the punches, ready to adapt to every circumstance, and respond to seize opportunities whenever they appear.

On the Means and Ends of Artistic Expression:
Bruce Lee: It is like a finger, pointing a way to the moon. Don't concentrate on the finger, or you will miss all that heavenly glory.

Trent Harris: Technique and individual performance are things that can help get you to magic and that transcendent state, but if you're thinking about them while you're playing, you're probably going to miss getting to the good stuff."

Functional MRI machines have shown that Jazz music and rap music use parts of our brains involved in conversation and the give-and-take of creating a dialogue. These areas are not involved in playing a memorized musical piece. Likewise, performing memorized martial arts techniques uses different parts of our brains than does creating free-form, spontaneous self-defense like we do in Systema. A big lesson here is that just practicing rote techniques more and more will not engage the part of our brains that generates creative self-defense against a live opponent.

Sadly, Bruce Lee's JKD has crystallized into a "style." Systema is still jazz, martial jazz at its finest.

Wrestling Alone

"It's not a wrestling match if only one person is wrestling."

⟹

In 1995 Robert Putnam wrote a book, Bowling Alone, in which he chronicled the decline of community and social activities in America. Factors like urban sprawl, high levels of divorce, declining membership in civic clubs and TV have led people to conduct their lives in increasing isolation, without ever interacting with other people. The sad imagery of a man bowling by himself because he has no friends aptly sums up the decline of strong social networks.

Wrestling — and the more combative term, grappling — has become synonymous with martial arts in America. Bowling alone may be depressing, but how could you even possibly wrestle alone? It's a zen koan, of the *"what's the sound of one hand clapping?"* variety. What would it mean to wrestle by yourself and what exactly would it look like?

I was teaching a ground-fighting class with the goal of teaching students to flow with their attackers, without tying up or locking themselves up. I noticed that one student, who came from a long wrestling background, was fighting against his opponent. He was clearly muscling everything and trying to "beat his opponent." He was a pretty good wrestler, but he was wearing himself out and not getting anywhere.

Off the cuff, I said to him, *"It's not a wrestling match if only one person is wrestling."* He immediately stopped and looked at me, perplexed. I seemed to be speaking a foreign language, and I watched him try to process what I just said. It took a physical demonstration/comparison of how he was moving versus good Systema movement for him to feel the difference between fighting and flowing.

I'm from Chicago, but I live in Colorado, land of the rodeo. There's not one cowboy, no matter how strong, who can hold on to a bucking bronco by trying to wrestle with it. Tense, struggling cowboys out of sync with the bucking are instantly and spectacularly launched into the air. In contrast, the best cowboys who stay atop these wild animals the longest are those who relax and move *with* the more powerful beast.

Systema ground work is akin to riding the bucking bronco more than it is trying to wrestle it to the ground. The grappler may wrestle and struggle, but Systema principles dictate that we relax and move with our opponent; we do not try to establish a position and defend it for points. Survival on the ground is not a sport freeing Systemists to work in ways that are effective for combat but that would force wrestlers to "lose points." To us, the fight is for our lives, not a trophy.

The key to proper ground work is that the irresistible force should meet the <u>moveable</u> object each and every time.

The Future of Systema

On my first trip to Russia, the Russian students were as unsure of us Americans as we were of them, due to lingering memories of the Cold War. Here they were, teaching combat secrets to us, Americans who had been painted as "the enemy" for their entire lives. Choosing partners felt a bit like a middle school dance with everyone a little hesitant to pick a partner.

The training started out fairly stern and serious, but within a few days training sessions were dominated by mutual smiles and friendly hugs; both sides worked to break the ice. One Russian student commented that the Russians didn't think Americans would "get" or even like Systema — a sentiment I could tell that they all shared at the beginning of our visit — but was pleasantly surprised at how well we worked and trained while in Russia.

Almost a decade and a half later, Systema training has exploded in America and all over the world thanks to Mikhail, Vladimir and a growing legion of instructors. Systema has gone from *"what the heck is that?"* to *"I've seen videos of that on the web"* and even *"I did a little Systema in another town.*" Systema has taken its rightful place among the other well-known martial arts from around the world. The question is, where does Systema go from here?

So it's time to pull out my crystal ball, consult the tea leaves, shuffle the tarot cards, read my palm, or whatever supposed psychics do to (allegedly) predict the future. OK, I can't predict the future, nor can you, so the best I can do is take a look at possible directions Systema could take.

1. Systema can go softer. The trend in martial arts and martial artists is that as they age they become softer and more spiritual/religious like Ueshiba did with his Aikido.
2. Systema can go the Tai Chi route and emphasize the health aspect of the art, at the expense of the combat aspect.
3. Systema can become the next major trend in martial arts as it infects other martial arts. It could go the route of *"I do X and also Systema,"* wherein people just take a part of Systema to improve their main martial art of study. It could be just another art added to the "JKD martial arts collection."
4. Systema can become more and more insular, divorced from other martial arts for fear of being tainted, or tested. Because tension and aggression are derided, Systema practitioners may prefer to work with only soft, passive partners instead of engaging and learning to work with the majority of martial artists and how they fight, tensely and aggressively.
5. Systema can go the military art route and focus on

weaponry and military applications. Modern Systema was forged in the Russian military so it may become a niched martial art with military-specific applications that civilians may not want to, or have need to, study.
6. Systema can adapt for sport and the MMA rage. As more MMA fighters cross-train in Systema, and vice versa, Systema may trend toward effectiveness in the cage. The relaxation, evasiveness, breathing and striking will enhance any art.

Systema really is doing all of these at once and will continue to do so. Such is the nature of an all-encompassing martial art like Systema that has infinite applications. Each person who becomes a certified instructor will apply Systema principles to his previous martial art and adapt it to his needs. Such radical individualism prevents any Systema orthodoxy of method. Systema is pluralistic at heart, with creative individuals leading the way for the next generations.

Long-term success and proliferation of Systema requires practitioners to continually re-create the conditions that created the art originally – a variety of inputs and martial arts methods to adapt to. Each Systemist must be exposed to the best martial arts techniques the world has ever seen, and be taught how to overcome them, which will certainly continue to produce Systemists with expert skill.

Systema as Asymptote

"Have no fear of perfection. You will never reach it."
— Salvador Dali

In high school geometry class, I was introduced to the concept of asymptotes for the first time. If you slept through geometry class or just forgot it all as soon as your final exam was over, here's a quick recap. An asymptote is a line associated with a curve in which the curve comes infinitely close to the line, although it never intersects the line. The curve never reaches the line as it moves to infinity.

In the martial arts, the asymptote is perfection. In Systema, that perfection refers to breathing, relaxation, movement and structure. Students and instructors are always striving to breathe efficiently, be more relaxed, move at the right time and have perfect form – something none of us can ever reach.

I have seen Systema teachers stop students from even beginning a self-defense move because they are tense. Of course, the students are tense. They are beginners and they are *learning*. Everyone is initially tense when they are learning something new. That's what it means to be a student. Graduating from being tense to being relaxed and fluid is a process. It is a process that teachers have to help students move successfully through, not stop them before they can even practice. How is a student supposed to smooth out his movements if he is continually castigated for being too tense? Teaching this way adds judgment and self-consciousness to his training. Demanding total, perfect relaxation before a student can move is futile. It's asymptotic.

My main criteria as a teacher is, *"did you defend yourself?"* (The purpose of self-defense training)

"Yes."

"Ok, let's work on being smoother and relaxing your shoulder now (or whatever needs improvement)."

I'd rather have a student who can defend himself, but has a little more tension than one who cannot defend himself and is totally relaxed. Systema is asymptotic in the quality of expressing its main principles, and it is asymptotic in the scope of its application.

Once I was talking to Vladimir about how cool Systema is (one of many conversations) after yet another of his "drinking from a fire hose" seminars. I told him that with other martial arts, the more I studied the less there seemed to be. Reading my mind, he picked up my train of thought and replied, *"And with Systema there is always more."* Exactly. After just about a decade and a half of Systema there's no end in sight. I can only see more to learn, not less. Systema is asymptotic in its breadth of applications. There are always more elements and different situations to apply the principles to. Just one example: how many martial arts have a system of fighting in and under water in addition to fighting on land?

None of us can perform Systema perfectly at all times and in all circumstances. While that may depress some, it is a relief and removes the burden of having to be the perfect teacher who never makes a mistake. Though we cannot reach the asymptote of perfection, how close we work to get to it will determine our ultimate success and happiness with ourselves.

What level of imperfection will you settle for?"
— Brandon Lee

I Can't Make This Stuff Up

When you've been teaching as long as I have you see some strange things, and some strange people (if one of the following people is you, yes, you are strange). None of them stick around for long. We either guide them out the door or they self-select out. Where these types come from I don't know, but Systema seems to attract a unique variety of strange. Their appearance at the school, and disappearance, sure do make for some good stories. Here are a few highlights:

Guy comes in, asks, *"Scornavacco? Are you Russian?"*
"No."
"Then how can you teach Russian Martial Art?"
"The same way I can cook Chinese food."

This guy comes to class, having looked up my school online; he even starts taking classes. In one class, I surprised him with a deep punch that put him on the floor. Afterward, he said that he has been writing critical remarks about the Russian government and wanted to know if "they" sent me to take him out.

Um, he looked me up and came to my school to train, I didn't seek him out. If he was so afraid of Russians out to get him, why did he decide to train at a *Russian* martial arts school?

This guy in his mid-20s comes in the door to train, saying that his "Master" was doing Systema — but didn't call it Systema — and so Andrew, The Student, wanted a certified teacher to train him. Of course, when word got back to The Master, also a twenty-something, he persuaded his girlfriend to buy him a few classes. In typical fashion, he was way too tense, couldn't breathe right and didn't move, so naturally, he got thrown around by everyone in class, including the beginners.

After class The Master reiterated, *"We're really doing the same thing, I just didn't know there was a name for it"* (not from where I was standing). We never saw him again.

This 19-year-old guy from Kansas with an MMA background comes to class when we happen to be doing takedown defense. He asks Joe Malglioglio (Systema instructor and former Golden Gloves Champ) what he would do if he tried to take him down, MMA-style.

Joe says, *"Let's see."*

So he tries to tackle Joe, who promptly punches him in the solar plexus, putting him on the floor.

After a few minutes trying to get his breath back, the guy gets back up and says, *"OK, what would you do if you didn't punch me in the solar plexus?"*

I used to put new students with one of my advanced students. That way the student would help the newbie while I taught the rest of the class. After having a few rough guys try out class I decided to work with the newbies myself so they wouldn't hurt my beginner students. I thought it was a nice gesture too.

So this Krav Maga guy comes in while we're doing knife work. We were doing a flow drill and he starts amping things up so I put him on the mat. He does this a few times with the same result. Meanwhile, I have students on either side watching this all go down.

Apparently this guy decides that more speed and more aggression is what he needs to work successfully. He loses it and goes full-speed, full-out attacking me. I don't remember how, but I put him on his face and held him down.

He says," *I don't understand what you want me to do?"*

To which I replied, *"I want you to calm down and slow down. Then I'll let you up."*

The last I heard from him, he'd given up martial arts and was in massage school.

This guy has been calling us every year for the past four years (I think he pencils us in on his calendar). He talks to my assistant, Michelle, and says the same thing each time.

"Systema looks fake, but I want to come to class and check it out."

Michelle, always gracious, invites him to try a class but he always makes excuses why he can't come to class.

Come to think of it, we are about due for another call from good old Chuck.

One new student was having a particularly difficult time grasping, rather, applying Systema in class. At our end of class Discussion Circle he left us with one of the best quotes ever, *"I don't understand. I've watched all the DVD's, why can't I do this?"*

Really? I'm shocked.

Guy comes to class, saying he teaches all sorts of martial arts and wants to learn Systema. Here we go again. He is stiff, immobile, holding his breath and always bending over. You know the routine by now. Everyone is tossing him around. He can't take a Systema punch.

At one point he said, *"I just spent a weekend doing this other kind of knife defense.*

So we show him what we would do to him if he tried those techniques with us (and we did).

Then he said, *"You mean I have to do the opposite of everything I just spent a weekend learning?"* (He's into weekend certification programs).

I said, "If you want to be good at Systema."

So he disappears. About a year later, I get an invitation to come train Systema with him — as in freely exchange ideas — because he has all the best DVD's. I'll work with anyone, but this guy couldn't hold up to students with one month of experience in my classes. I'd never call Vladimir, even after all these years, and invite him to come workout with me. Good grief.

What we consider relaxed is much different than what people from other martial arts see as relaxed. These guys come to a few classes and learn the smallest sliver of Systema. All of a sudden you'd think they are GrandMasters by reading how they describe themselves. They are so radically different and better now.

Does it ever occur to them that if they got this good with just three Systema classes, then how much better someone who regularly attends classes would be, much less what someone with over a decade of Systema would be? It reminds me of the guys who learn a 6-count stick drill and think they are professional stick fighters or the guys who learn how to escape the mount and think they are world-class grapplers. By comparison, it takes several months to earn a Yellow Belt, the first rank in many martial arts systems.

I was teaching a class on how to take down an attacker who is resisting. This guy comes to class and is paired with David (who makes his living as The Zip Code Man, a street performer who tells you what zip code you live in when you tell him the name of the city). He tells David he can't be knocked over. He says, *"You can't move me when I'm rooted to Mother Earth."*

So David says, *"oh really?"* and proceeds to toss him into the weapons rack.

Poor guy. No one told him we don't really have roots.

This Krav Maga guy happens to come into a class on striking. He tells me that he is recovering from having his ribs broken in his KM class.

So I asked him, *"Did they teach you to move?"*

"Huh?"

So I have him punch me as I demonstrate how to move and dissipate the energy of the punch.

He said, *"Uh, no, I had to just stand there and take it."*

I said, *"Does that seem like a good idea?"*

"No, now that I think about it."

This woman, a 5th Degree TKD Black Belt comes to a workshop and has a heck of a time picking up Systema. Finally, she has a meltdown. She breaks down and says, *"I just can't do this. I can teach people how to do a side kick but I CAN'T DO THIS. Why can't I do this?"*

Well, the short answer is these are very different skills.

Systema is great because it runs the gamut from soft & flowing to downright brutal. For awhile I thought/knew that the striking was scaring away new students so I decided to emphasize the flowing aspects of the art to a pair of newbies.

I CAN'T MAKE THIS STUFF UP

We have a great class, moving, flowing, escaping and putting attackers down. It is fun work all around.

So after an hour and a half of this, the guys say, *"We thought there would be more hitting."*

So I grab one of the guys and show them how we hit each other and what Systema striking is like. I see their wide-eyed stares and say, *"Would you guys like to try this?"*

"Uh, that's ok," they say as they hurry out the door.

Sometimes you just can't win.

You just never know. I was invited by a fellow instructor to teach a workshop on striking to validate Systema striking because, get this, who would believe that someone my size could hit that hard?

I went far out of my way to take this group by the hand and walk them step-by-step through striking practice, with painstaking detail. The biggest guy in the room volunteers to get struck. By the end he's hugging me, saying how great he feels, so I'm thinking, "success."

He doesn't come back the next day. I heard that he had to go to a body-worker because of all the negative energy coming out of him — something I warned him about, that striking brings up pent-up emotions. They will never have me back to teach and instead opted to have my friend Martin Wheeler because *"Brad's too brutal."*

Really? I'm the least intimidating person in this whole art.

Guy comes in, wants to check out class. I sense immediately

that he doesn't want to take class, just talk. So he tells me he's Russian Orthodox Christian and wants to talk about the Systema connection.

At one point he said, *"I'm a deacon, and I'm the number one sinner."*

I said, *"Maybe I should call the police then."*

Never saw him again.

During a striking class I punched a student in the kidney. He said, *"Ow, it hurts getting punched in the kidney."*

I said, *"Don't worry, you have another one."*

He pulled up his shirt, revealing a scar, *"No, I don't."*

Strike responsibly.

Systema Everywhere

The current rage in popular science is "neuro." Everything now is brain-based: neuro-economics, neuro-marketing, neuro-parenting. If you put the word neuro in front of any word you are sure to get attention. All hail the nervous system.

Neuro-plasticity, as popularized in Norman Doidge's book The Brain That Changes Itself, refers to the fact that our brains wire and re-wire themselves with experience. The idea is earth-shattering, but Steven Pinker put it in its proper perspective, *"that's just a way of saying that we can learn. If the brain didn't change, we couldn't learn (sic)."* Brilliant!

So everything we learn physically changes our brains. I am a pianist so my brain is different from a violinist's brain. I would show more growth in regions involving use of both my hands, while a violinist would only show growth in regions involving use of the left hand, which does the intricate work on the strings. Every brain is unique due to our unique experiences.

Doing Systema changes our brains, so we literally become different people from the people we were when we started training. We sense, think and feel in new, more efficient ways due to our Systema training. In a very real sense, our decision to train in Systema has put us on a different course and changed our lives.

Years ago, Mikhail was explaining how to perform Systema. He said, *"You should do Systema like you butter your toast."* This analogy has made the rounds online, but what people miss was Mikhail's perfect impersonation of Samurai Delicatessen, John Belushi's skit from Saturday Night Live (At least that's who he reminded me of). His ludicrous portrayal of attacking a piece of toast hammered the point home that we should do Systema the same way we perform everyday tasks.

While most of us butter our toast effortlessly (sorry for the grain analogy Paleo-people), many of us go through life with far too much tension. People walk into the bank like they are going to war, rather than just making a deposit. This analogy does go both ways — as Systema changes our brains and bodies, our graceful movements in class should pervade the rest of our lives and all of our movements, no matter where we are. Systema makes us more relaxed and more efficient every day, in every way. In fact, my students regularly report how they have reduced tension in their daily lives, such as holding the steering wheel with relaxed shoulders, sitting at their desks with better posture and dealing non-violently with interpersonal conflicts.

So, do Systema like you butter your toast, and butter your toast like you do Systema.

"There's more to life than Systema."
-Valerie Vasiliev

Quotes from Class

Students often verbalize their training experiences as they try to process the day's lesson. Here are some insightful comments, some bits of dialogue between training partners, as well as some of my explanations.

"It always works when I do it the way you tell us to."

"Systema doesn't work? Not the way you're doing it."

"If you're not hitting your partner, you're not helping your partner."

"It's all fake...until you get hit"

"Every time you touch 'em it should hurt."

"You should be able to touch them without their knowing it."

"Think globally, strike locally"

"Usually when you break his arm he drops the knife."

"It's amazing how much energy you don't need to do this right."

"In this class, it's not 'who broke your rib?' it's 'how did you allow your rib to get broken?'"

"It's so much easier when you do it right."

"Doing Systema is like being a bad dance partner."

"That's just not fair."

"Name one skill that couldn't be improved by proper breathing, more relaxed movement and proper body alignment."

"That was surprisingly easy."

"The curse of the mediocre is thinking they are exceptional, the burden of the exceptional is dealing with the mediocre. A little knowledge inflates the ego."

"I just want to escape."
Good, just take him (the attacker) with you."

"But I still have the knife."
"And you have a broken neck."

QUOTES FROM CLASS | 215

"This is hard."
"I never said it was easy, I just said to do it."

"Move, escape."
"Can't I just punch him?"

"Belts and Sticks? Can't we just do chains and whips?"

"Why don't they do this in Jiu-Jitsu?"
"We do Systema here."

"Why don't they do this in my school?"
"I don't know. I don't go to your school."

Acknowledgements

If you haven't written a book you might think the author just sits down, types and voila! There's a book.

Actually, writing a book is a bit like moving. You move out all the furniture: the couches, tables and chairs and you think you are done because you've done all the heavy lifting. Then you turn around, look into the house and see all the "stuff" still left to move out. Every last piece of "stuff" has to be moved until every room is 100% empty. The main bulk of the writing is just the first step toward getting a real book completed.

I'm very big picture-oriented and dealing with the small details is about as much fun having my chest hairs ripped out by my 2-year old daughter. That being said, I have many people to thank for this book winding up in your hands.

Thanks to Paul Trout for reading, editing and finding time to write the foreword.

Thanks to Stephen Weiner for editing this book.

Thanks to Eduardo Soto for his amazing cover design.

Thanks to Al McLuckie for loaning me his masterful oil

painter's eye and suggesting the finishing touches to the cover that make it so striking.

Thanks to Mikhail Ryabko and Vladimir Vasiliev for sharing this awe-inspiring martial art with me.

Thanks to all my Systema instructor friends who I look forward to seeing, no matter what city it is we all have to travel to in order to sweat together. Great times, always. I look forward to next time, every time.

Thanks to my students for their questions, challenges and mistakes, without which this book never would have been written.

Thanks Mom and Dad for supporting me in a lifetime of what I'm sure seemed like crazy decisions at the time. *"You're going where? Moscow to train with the Russian Military? Ok, have fun."* :)

Thanks to my wonderful wife, Karla, for always being there for me.

Kids, this one's for you.

Visit www.SystemaColorado.com for Brad's Scornavacco's highly acclaimed collection of training videos, WarriorFit program, books and articles.

To host or attend training workshops with Brad please call 303-485-5425 or email office@scornavacco.com

Visit our YouTube Channel, SystemaColorado.

About the Author

Brad Scornavacco is one of the longest-time, continually teaching Certified Systema Instructors in the United States and is one of the first Americans to travel to Russia to train directly with Systema Master Mikhail Ryabko. In 2003, he demonstrated Systema for the Russian Minister of the Interior, where the current Ryabko-lineage Systema logo was unveiled. Brad appeared with Mikhail, Vladimir and other top Systema teachers on Russian television.

Brad grew up in the Back of the Yards neighborhood on the South Side of Chicago and — being a small kid in a big city — learned first-hand the need for practical, realistic self-defense. Brad began his martial arts training in 1984 in Ed Parker Kenpo (and later, Tai Chi) under Lee Wedlake Jr. He trained in Filipino and Indonesian Martial Arts with a variety of teachers, including Huk Planas and Edgar Sulite. He holds Guro (teacher) certification in Al McLuckie's Filipino Warrior Arts. He began training in Mixed Martial Arts in 1993 (before the term existed). All of these "reality-based" martial arts led him ultimately to the Russian Martial Art.

Brad moved to Colorado and opened Scornavacco Martial Arts Academy in 1998 in Longmont, where he teaches this variety of martial arts to children and adults.

A graduate of Northwestern University with Degrees in Philosophy and Economics, Brad draws from a strong foundation in peak mind/body performance to offer his students a once-in-a-lifetime experience of learning from a unique instructor who others call *"the best teacher I've ever had"* as well as *"the one who truly models and explains what is going on"* with powerful, complex martial arts such as Systema.

Brad is the creator of the *WarriorFit® Portable Personal Training System*, and is the author of *The Consumer's Guide to Choosing the Right Martial Arts School*. Brad teaches Systema around the world and makes his teaching available through his highly acclaimed DVD series.

CPSIA information can be obtained at www.ICGtesting.com
Printed in the USA
BVOW080954010513

319569BV00001B/148/P

9 781478 717805